SMART WOMEN
THROUGHOUT HISTORY

INTELLIGENT WOMEN WHO DID GREAT THINGS

CHRISTINE BENNET

www.christinebennet.com

www.flyingcatbooks.com

To all the women who allow their imagination,
intelligence and commit
to guide them to
new ideas.

NO PLACE FOR A WOMAN SERIES

Adventurous Women Throughout History:
Women In History That Other Women Should Read About

Royal Women Throughout History:
Biographies About Royal Women From All Different Countries
Through The Ages

Musical Women Throughout History:
The Women Who Fought For Music

Smart Women Throughout History:
Intelligent Women Who Had Great Ideas

CONTENTS

.

INTRODUCTION

Some of the most remarkable stories of survival, perseverance, and bravery come from women in history. Society has always been quick to diminish the achievements and intelligence of women, although women have always risen above to prove that they are just as (if not more) powerful and amazing as men. In this edition of the *No Place for a Woman* series, I will focus on the stories of some incredibly smart women who changed the world. Their contributions to society are immeasurable, and the world would be a very different place if it weren't for their intelligence and tenacity.

As modern women, we can look at those who paved the way for us and take inspiration from their strength and bravery. No matter what struggle you are going through in life, there will always be tales of inspirational events that can bolster your confidence and keep you going. Regardless of what is happening in your own life, you will be able to find parallels and tidbits that relate to what you are going through. As you read through the history and achievements of these women, you will see how many of their struggles speak directly to your own experience, and more importantly, you'll see facets of the strength you hold within you reflected in their tales.

In this book, you will find the stories of women such as Caroline Herschel, the first professional female astronomer, who made waves in the 18th century. You will also read about one of the biggest names in the history of literature, Jane Austen. Then, there is famed mathematician and computer programmer Ada Lovelace and Victorian-era biologist Marianne North. I'll also explore the life of Rebecca Lee Crumpler, the first African American woman to become a doctor, as well as multi-talented author, illustrator, naturalist, and conservationist Beatrix Potter. You undoubtedly have heard the name Marie Curie, and I'll take the time to outline her contribution to science. There is the interesting story of Maria Montessori, a woman who changed the world of education, and Joan Beauchamp, who shaped the study of zoology. I'll delve into the life of computer scientist and military woman Grace Hopper. I'll then tell the story of the fascinating Hedy Lamarr, without whom we wouldn't have Wi-Fi, and finish with the life of Maree Van Brittan Brown, who shaped the world of home security systems.

All these women made unfathomable changes to the world, and the road wasn't easy for them. They all came up against countless hurdles, from sexism to racism; they had to fight for their voices to be heard. To this day, their contributions are often overshadowed by their male contemporaries, which is why it is so important to tell their stories.

Personally, researching and learning about the women in this book provided me with so much inspiration that I now feel like a new woman. I feel stronger and braver, and I know their stories will have the same effect on you. The women who came before us struggled and overcame adversity so that we could learn from them. They left us with a blueprint for how to be successful in the face of what the world throws at us and proved that women are the strongest people in the world.

I have no doubt that you are currently battling with challenges that seem too big to bear. I've been in your position. I've dealt with many, *many* obstacles that I wasn't sure I could overcome, and by looking at the stories of women who came before me, I found the strength I needed to just keep going—and so can you. So, please join me as I explore the lives of some of the smartest women in history!

1

———◦———

CAROLINE HERSCHEL (1750–1845)

FIRST WOMAN ASTRONOMER

Caroline Herschel is a name you may have never heard before. She is often overshadowed by her older brother, William Herschel, although without Caroline, even his name would be lost to history. Alongside William, Caroline is credited with the discovery of many comets, and without her, he would have never discovered the planet Uranus. Without Caroline, important astronomical findings may have taken centuries to be uncovered. She was the world's first professional female astronomer and the first woman to be awarded the prestigious Gold Medal of the Royal Astronomical Society. She made it possible for generations of women to pursue careers in the field of astronomy and serves as an inspiration for millions of girls who are interested in astrophysics.

Even in today's day and age, the scientific world is heavily male-dominated, so you can only imagine how difficult it would have been for a woman to become an astronomer in the 18th and early 19th centuries. In both Germany and England, where Caroline lived, women were heavily oppressed. The main job for a woman was to be a homemaker and to breed and take care of children. They were expected to tend to their husband's needs, with little to no time left to engage with their own interests or things that gave them pleasure. Few women had paying jobs, and if they did work, their occupations were limited to positions such as cooks or cleaners. Notably, though, during this time in history, some women started to receive education—though it was usually minimal. Middle and upper-class girls were given lessons in basic reading and writing skills, although it was deemed useless to teach them complex subjects like advanced mathematics and advanced literature (Stiller, 2023). Instead,

3

their studies focused on "feminine" subjects like needlework and dance. If girls did receive a higher education, it was customary for them to downplay their intelligence so they could be perceived as "marriageable." Not only that, it was also commonly believed that women were fundamentally less intelligent than men due to a theory regarding the size difference between the brains of the two sexes, suggesting females were less clever. With this in mind, as well as the disparity in the quality of education between men and women, it is no wonder that scientists and mathematicians were exclusively male.

Looking at the historical context of her life, it is even more amazing that Caroline Herschel achieved what she did in such an oppressive and sexist period. Not only did she have to prove to men that she was intelligent, she also had personal struggles to overcome. She was a sickly child, and some of her health issues plagued her well into adulthood. A less tenacious person might have given up on pursuing their interests, but lucky for us, Caroline was never going to stop pushing. She had a desire to learn about the world, even if it left her a social outcast.

Caroline's life story reminds me that no matter your circumstances and how impossible things seem, if you want to do something, you just have to keep going. She wasn't born into a world that celebrated female intelligence or into a wealthy family that made it easy for her to gain an education. She had to battle debilitating health issues and lived with a disability in an era where differently abled people (especially women) were considered worthless. The odds were well and truly stacked against her— she rose above her challenges and became a pioneer.

You might recognize a few of Caroline's struggles from your own life. I'd hazard a guess that you've dealt with sexism many times in your life. If you live with any disability, I'm sure you can empathize with how difficult it was for her to adjust and overcome this hurdle. As you read Caroline's story, I hope you gain inspiration from her perseverance and remember that you, too, have the strength to achieve your goals, regardless of how hard life may seem.

A Brief History

Caroline Lucretia Herschel was born on the 16th of March 1750 in Hanover, Germany (then the Holy Roman Empire). Her father, Issak Herschel, was a self-taught oboe player and her mother, Anna Ilse Moritzen, was a homemaker. She was the couple's eighth child. Prior to her birth, her father was a bandmaster in the army, and while away at war he fell ill, which resulted in chronic pain and incurable asthma. Due to his illness, he spent much of his time at home. Issak Herschel was passionate about educating all his children—even his daughters. While he did want Caroline to be educated, the pressures of running a household got in the way. When her older sister Sophia married and moved away, Caroline was the only daughter left in the house, and household labor expectations fell on her at the age of only five. She was able to partake in far fewer lessons than her brothers, only learning the basics of reading and writing while juggling her other tasks.

All hopes of an equal education came to a halt when Caroline was 10. She fell incredibly ill, suffering from a typhus infection that impacted the rest of her life. The severity of the illness permanently stunted her growth, meaning she never grew taller than four feet and three inches. For context, this is the average height for a modern-day eight-year-old child. She also lost some vision in her left eye, which plagued her for the rest of her life (Ogilvie, 2011). This wasn't the first health condition that impacted Caroline's life; at age three, she had contracted smallpox, which left her face marked with scars. Due to her frail appearance and vision issues, her family concluded that she would never marry, which meant that she would need to work to sustain herself.

While Caroline's father expressed wishes for his daughter to be tutored, her mother, Anna, was deeply opposed, especially after Caroline fell ill. Anna wanted her to focus on learning how to be a house servant and forbade her from taking any irrelevant lessons. Issak didn't agree with his wife, and whenever Anna was away from the family home, he would include Caroline in tutoring sessions with her brothers, where she picked up a little more knowledge about the world and even learned to play the violin. However, she primarily spent her childhood learning dressmaking and needlework.

After her father passed away, Caroline's older brother William implored her to move to Bath, England and join them as a singer. He was working as a church performer and wanted to get his sister away from their oppressive mother, who had the steadfast belief that Caroline's destiny was to be a house servant and nothing more (Hoskin, 2014). In 1772 at age 22, Caroline left Hanover to see how different her life could be away from the family home. It was thanks to William that this was possible. He came back to Germany to collect his sister and paid his mother to release her from her servant duties.

This journey from Hanover to Bath was of paramount importance to the trajectory of Caroline's life. It was during this trip that she first became interested in astronomy. At the time, she was just fascinated with how different constellations would appear. Little did she know this budding curiosity would transform her life.

CAROLINE AND WILLIAM

Caroline's life in Bath was both fortunate and difficult. No longer confined to the rigorous rules of her mother, she had to adapt to a whole new world. She took on the responsibilities of running her brother's household alone. While this would have been more than enough work to keep her occupied, William didn't want his sister to lead a simple life. After all, he had invited her to the city to perform with him, so he started to give her singing lessons. He also tutored her in English and mathematics at any available hour. William himself was busy. He had made a name for himself as an organist and music teacher, as well as working as the choirmaster at a Bath chapel. He was quickly becoming an in-demand musician and was frequently requested for public concerts. When William was unable to keep up privately tutoring Caroline, she began to take singing and dancing lessons from a local teacher and learned to play the harpsichord.

While free and able to do (mostly) as she pleased, Caroline led a lonely life in Bath. She found it difficult to make friends, and it is likely that the locals were unwilling to accept her because she looked different and sickly (Fernie, 2007). We all have an underlying need to belong to a community, so this would have undoubtedly impacted Caroline's happiness, although she didn't let it stop her from pursuing other things that could bring her joy. She dove headfirst into her studies and took every opportunity she was given to make a better life for herself.

With her brother by her side, Caroline started to also make a name for herself in the music scene. She became the principal singer at his concerts, and people started to notice that the female Herschel was also talented. Other conductors began to offer her roles as a soloist, although she declined to perform with anybody other than William.

Caroline felt forever indebted to William, to the point where when his interest shifted from music to astronomy, she supported him—though she wasn't entirely happy about it. She wanted to continue her career as a professional singer although put that aside to help William as he delved into a new field. When reflecting on this transition, Caroline wrote in her memoir, "I did nothing for my brother but what a well-trained puppy dog would have done, that is to say, I did what he commanded me" (Herschel, 1876). While that quote is pretty bitter, she did also credit her brother with releasing her from the monotony of female duties, which is ultimately why she stayed loyal and never struck out on her own as a performer.

So, somewhat begrudgingly, Caroline began to assist William with his astronomy research in the late 1770s. Caroline would grow to love studying the universe, and her ability to bring out the best in her brother resulted in the Herschel name forever being synonymous with astronomical discoveries.

CAROLINE AND ASTRONOMY

While still performing music regularly, William started to dabble with astronomy and began building his own telescopes. He found that he was unhappy with the quality of telescopes he could purchase and wanted to create a better instrument for research. This started to take over his life, and it fell on Caroline to care for her brother. She would regularly have to physically feed him, forcing food into his mouth while he worked. He would work almost 16 hours straight, attempting to construct a reflecting telescope. He also began corresponding with other scientists, including Sir William Watson, who invited William to join the Bath Philosophical Society. This invitation led to William gaining even more contacts in the astronomy world.

William was learning quickly, and so was Caroline. She began to copy astronomical papers and other publications, reading and recording their findings, then dictating them to her brother as he worked. She also started to organize and catalog her brother's observations so that it would be easier to sift through the data. Caroline had to learn all of this on her feet, as she didn't have any formal training, and all her education on mathematics had come from what William could teach her; many would have crumbled under the pressure of picking up something so quickly, although Caroline was so intelligent that it didn't faze her. She had to be quick, precise, and accurate at all times and never failed to keep up with her brother's discoveries and theories.

The brother-sister duo was knee-deep in astronomy, and if it were up to William, they probably would have starved to death before making any significant contribution. Caroline had to ensure that they had enough money not only to sustain their lifestyle and to be able to purchase parts for William's telescopes. They continued to perform in Bath and surrounding towns; however, their abilities weren't what they used to be. No doubt exhausted and preoccupied, their music suffered and was critically panned (Hoskin, 2014).

Uranus

The Herschel siblings' "big break" (so to speak) came on the 13th of March 1781, when William spotted what he thought was an undiscovered comet or stellar disc. He took a report of his sighting to the Astronomer Royal (the lead astronomer for the British Royal Family) and continued to track it. Additional research was conducted by Russian astronomer Anders Lexell, and the joint information led to the conclusion that this unidentified object must be a planet.

William began referring to this planet as the "Georgian Star" after the ruling monarch King George III. French astronomers began calling it "Herschel," which was a name that stuck for many decades in non-Commonwealth countries, catapulting the Herschel name into mass recognition. It wasn't renamed as "Uranus" until 1850.

In the wake of this massive discovery, William was appointed "The King's Astronomer" in 1782 and was elected a Fellow of the Royal Society (Clerke, 2010). This new role and prestige meant that the Herschels no longer needed to continue performing. They gave their last performance in that same year and began focusing all their attention on astronomy.

Part of his job as "The King's Astronomer" was to entertain royal guests. Caroline and William moved away from the busy city of Bath to the small town of Datchet, which is close to Windsor Castle, making it easier for them to perform their duties. Caroline was devastated to leave. Despite struggling to fit in for many years, she had finally made friends and adored the culture of the city, especially the music scene. In her memoir, she described their new house as being "in a deplorably ruinous condition, with harden and grounds overgrown with weeds" (Herschel, 1876).

Her job as William's unofficial assistant was to hire and supervise domestic servants, prepare the house for guests, and stay on top of her brother's work with an even more stringent need for attention to detail now that the King was involved. When William began the difficult task of cataloging 3,000 stars, specifically focusing on the phenomenon of double stars, he asked his sister to complete "sweeps" of the sky. This involved Caroline sitting at a telescope for hours, meticulously looking at the sky section by section to see if there were any interesting objects. This became her full-time job, and at first, she hated it. However, when she started to make discoveries of her own, she changed her tune. She reflected on this, writing (Herschel, 1876):

I was to be trained for an assistant astronomer; and by way of encouragement a telescope adapted for sweeping was given to me. I was to sweep for comets... But it was not till the last two months of the same year before I felt the least encouragement for spending the starlight nights on a grass-plot covered by dew or hoar frost without a human being near enough to be within call.

Her Own Discoveries

So, Caroline didn't love "sweeping" at first, and I don't blame her. I think we can all agree that it sounds a bit dull. She could have given up and moved back to Bath or done something else with her time, although her loyalty to William was too strong. This whole exercise could have resulted in nothing more than wasted time, and in the hands of a less intelligent person, it might have been just that. This was Caroline Herschel. She was always going to make the best of it. She did.

Less than a year after their move and a mere few months into sweeping, Caroline discovered her first open cluster, which is now called NGC 2360. Within the same year, she discovered a nebula that had never been documented before. She would go on to discover a total of 14 new nebulae. Impressed with her skill, William built Caroline her own telescope, specifically designed to search for comets. The two would work side by side, calling out potential findings to one another.

On the 1st of August 1686, at age 36, Caroline cemented herself as one of the most important women in scientific history. She became the first-ever woman to discover a comet. She didn't stop there. In 1788, she discovered her second comet, and her discovery was acknowledged and celebrated by the Astronomer Royal. She discovered two more comets in 1790 and garnered attention from famous naturalist and scientist Sir Joseph Banks. The following year, she made her fifth and sixth discoveries of two more comets. By 1797, she was credited for the discovery of a total of eight comets. Due to her outstanding contribution to the astronomical field, she was awarded an annual salary of £50 by the monarchy for her work as her brother's assistant (this equates to roughly £6,800, or around $8,100, today). She was the first woman to ever be paid as an astronomer, and the recognition of her as William's official assistant made her the first woman to ever be awarded an official government position in England (Lemonick, 2009).

In collaboration with her brother, Caroline began researching previous findings by John Flamsteed, who was the Astronomer Royal in the 1670s. They found that his published works contained many errors and concluded that his work needed to be cross-referenced. Caroline was tasked with the project and spent 20 months meticulously researching every observation made by John Flamsteed, outlining his errors and cataloging a list of more than 560 stars that he had failed to note (Hoskin, 2014). Despite the fact that it was Caroline who primarily worked on this research, the catalog was published under William's name in 1802 by the Royal Society. It became the reference point for all future astronomers, and to this day, many non-stellar objects are identified by the system Caroline created, now named the New General Catalogue (NGC).

An Astronomer Till the End

When William passed away in 1822, Caroline moved back to Hanover to deal with the grief of losing her closest collaborator and beloved brother. She continued to work as an astronomer, spending years confirming and producing evidence to corroborate the findings her brother had made during his career. She also kept working on the catalog and, in 1828, was awarded the Royal Astronomical Society's Gold Medal for her work. She was the first woman to ever receive the medal. Notably, it wasn't until 1996 that the award was given to a woman again—168 years after Caroline (Holmes, 2009).

Caroline continued working well into her 70s. She spent the last years of her life working alongside William's son, John Herschel, to assist him with his own astronomical findings. Thanks to the guiding hand of his aunt, John would go on to become an esteemed astronomer himself, also winning the Royal Astronomical Society's Gold Medal in 1826.

Right up until her death in 1848 at age 97, Caroline wrote papers and memoirs, socialized with great scientists, and remained an active figure in the astronomy world. She was buried next to her parents in Hanover, and her tombstone reads, "The eyes of her who is glorified here below turned to the starry heavens" (Redd, 2012).

CAROLINE'S LEGACY

The world of astronomy will forever be indebted to Caroline Herschel. Her dedication and sheer talent pushed forward some truly significant astronomical discoveries. Over the course of her life, she discovered over 2,400 astronomical objects (Hoskin, 2014). In her honor, an asteroid discovered in 1888 was named after her middle name—asteroid 281 Lucretia. Additionally, a crater on the moon was named C. Herschel in 1924. In 2020, a satellite named "Caroline" was launched into space.

In recent years, Caroline's legacy has repeatedly been recognized. In 2016, Google honored her birthday as part of their "Google Doodle" series, and in 2022 her memoirs were put on display at the Herschel Museum in Bath. Countless articles online list her as one of the most important women in science, so even though she had previously been overlooked because of her brother, the tides have already begun shifting so that people remember her in her own right.

What astounds me most about Caroline's story is that the odds were never in her favor. She was a sick child, she lived with physical disabilities, and she never received any formal education. There are very few people in the world who could become astronomy experts without years of studying the subject, although Caroline's intelligence and drive set her apart from the rest. She put her heart and soul into astronomy, even though it wasn't originally the career she wanted. As a woman, she knew she would potentially never receive any recognition for her work, although that didn't deter her. Caroline overcame obstacle after obstacle, kept her nose to the grindstone and worked hard, and stayed true to her work ethic no matter what. Her grit is an inspiration to us all. Regardless of what challenges are in your way, if you want to excel at something, you have the power within you to do it.

2

---◦◦◦---

JANE AUSTEN (1775–1817)

"BY A LADY"

You'd be hard-pressed to find a single adult in the English-speaking world who doesn't know the name Jane Austen. Her novels have stood the test of time, with millions of high school and college students studying her work. Lovers of literature are in awe of the tales she wrote, and there are at least 30 movies inspired by her stories. Even if you haven't read *Pride and Prejudice*, I'm sure you've seen at least one adaptation of the story in your life. Indeed, Jane Austen is perhaps the most famous female author of all time. It is estimated that over 30 million copies of her books have been sold worldwide (Curcic, 2022). She proved that you don't have to be a man to be a good writer, and it goes without saying that female authors have looked to Jane for inspiration for the last 200 years.

The topics of Jane's books often critique the societal norms of the era she was raised in. Similarly to Caroline Herschel, Jane lived in a time when the singular role of a woman was to answer to men. It was of paramount importance for women to marry, as they could not own land, earn an independent income, and often couldn't travel freely without a male escort. As soon as a young woman turned 15, her parents would begin to search for a husband for her. Girls had to conform to stringent societal expectations so that they would be seen as worthy of marriage. They needed to be demure and complacent—the worst thing for a girl in this era was to be viewed as rebellious or outspoken. In fact, one of the key markers of a "marriageable" girl was an "agreeable voice" (Walton, 2014). For women of all statuses, it was important that they possessed the skill of "running a household." They would be responsible for cooking, cleaning, and raising children, so, if they wanted to have a competitive edge and win a husband, they had to prove they were fit for the role. Upper-class women had to prove that they had the ability to manage domestic servants, as well as knowing how to entertain guests in their homes. Beauty standards are certainly not a modern convention and were just as important in the late 1700s. Girls who were deemed attractive had a better chance of finding a husband, and youthfulness was revered, which meant that families tried to marry off their daughters as soon as possible. While romantic ideations had started to gain popularity, it was still incredibly common for fathers to organize arranged marriages, and girls were often partnered with men over 10 years their senior. Once married, the women would essentially be the property of their husbands, with almost no chance of separation or divorce. With this in mind, it is no surprise that women were seldom able to pursue their passions and talents. Their job was to be a wife and mother—nothing more.

Jane Austen was ardently against this construct. She was a well-read and intelligent woman who knew that she was capable of much more. From an early age, she loved writing. Her letters to family and friends show that she wasn't meek or complacent she was rather a "very sharp-witted and at times rather acid-tongued woman" (NPR, 2010).

Jane didn't have any female influences to guide her. Female authors were practically nonexistent, though that didn't stop her from pursuing her passion. She proved that if you want to do something that's never been done before, all you need is bravery and tenacity, and you'll get it done. It wasn't necessarily Jane's goal to be a famous writer. She just did what brought her happiness—and we should all do the same. During her lifetime her work wasn't published under her name, and yet, she kept writing.

All this is to say that Jane's story teaches us that we should always do what we love and enjoy, even if nothing comes of it. It isn't important to be recognized or acclaimed. If you want to do it, then don't let anything stop you.

A Brief History

Jane Austen was born in Steventon, Hampshire in England on the 16th of December 1775. Her father, George Austen, was an Anglican clergyman, and her mother, Cassandra Leigh Austen, cared for the family. Cassandra Leigh was from a prominent family, though the majority of the inheritance from her parents was given to her older brother. George worked as a rector and took on boys to tutor and board to supplement the family income. Jane was the seventh of eight children.

Jane's early childhood has been referred to as "intellectually active" (Kennedy, 2019). She and her siblings would frequent their father's extensive library to read and would often put on theatrical performances for their parents. Jane was also a keen dancer and enjoyed attending balls held in the local town hall. Jane and her older sister Cassandra were educated at home at first, then in 1782, sent to study with their aunt in Southampton. They were sent home a year later after they both contracted typhus. Jane was so sick that she nearly died from the illness.

In 1784, Cassandra and Jane were sent to a boarding school in Reading, where they were taught writing, French, dance, music, drama, and needlework. Less than two years later, the sisters were forced to return home as the fees of the boarding school became too expensive for the family. They were then tutored at home by their father and brothers, and it is believed that they received an education similar to young boys rather than the simple lessons given to girls their age.

At age 11, Jane started to experiment with writing. Her father was tolerant of her interest, and she penned poems and short stories to entertain herself and her family. She was risque with her topics, however, writing about female empowerment and boisterous behavior. Between 1787 and 1793, Jane wrote at least 29 works, which have since been bound together into a collection called *Juvenilia* (Sutherland, 2014).

This was just the start for Jane. She didn't know that something she purely found pleasure in would result in her becoming one of the most recognizable names in the history of literature.

JANE AND WRITING

One of the pieces that Jane wrote that is now a part of *Juvenilia* was a satirical piece called *Love and Friendship* which she wrote at age 14. In this, she mocked the exceedingly popular books of the time that focused on sensibility. The following year she wrote *The History of England* in collaboration with her sister Cassandra, who illustrated watercolor pictures to accompany the story. At 18, she began working on her most sophisticated piece yet, a book titled *Lady Susan*, which took her two years to complete. This is considered to be her first proper novel, though there are no surviving copies of the original manuscript. It is believed that much of the contents of *Lady Susan* were used in her famed novel *Sense and Sensibility*, which was anonymously published many years later in 1811.

In 1796, Jane began working on her second novel, *First Impressions*, which would go on to be published under the title *Pride and Prejudice*—arguably her most famous novel of all time. She was only 21 at the time, and it is astounding that someone so young could write such an influential story that would be revered for centuries. Jane's goal when writing was simply to provide entertainment for her family, and they were all huge fans of this novel, immediately recognizing it as a great piece of writing. Her father even attempted to get the novel published, sending it to prolific publisher Thomas Cadell in London. Unfortunately, he was not successful, and the book fell by the wayside.

Undeterred, Jane kept writing, finishing her novel *Elinor and Marianne* in 1797, and going on to write another now-popular novel, *Northanger Abbey*. *Northanger Abbey* provides a nice insight into what Jane's personality was like. The book was written as a satire on the popular genre of the Gothic novel. Throughout her pieces, she often made fun of fashionable literature trends and societal expectations. Again, as she wasn't writing for anything more than pleasure and entertainment for people she was close to, she wasn't concerned with backlash and simply did as she pleased.

Bath and the Lost Years

In 1800, George Austen moved the family to Bath. This shock move heavily impacted a now 25-year-old Jane, who felt that the new city hampered her creativity. She spent some time tinkering with *Lady Susan* and embarked on a new novel titled *The Watsons*, which told the story of a heroine named Emma and explored Emma's relationship with her sisters. Still hampered by writer's block, the book was never finished, although the original manuscript survived. In 2014, novelist Ann Mychal wrote *Emma and Elizabeth*, inspired by the story Jane half-finished. Then in 2018, playwright Laura Wade adapted the unfinished work into a critically acclaimed stage play by the same name, which was performed on the West End in London for two years (Gans, 2019).

Jane Austen researchers believe that Jane lost interest in writing over this time because she became consumed by the social life in Bath (Irvine, 2005). She had previously lived in a relatively small place, and as I mentioned before, she was a huge fan of attending balls, so now that she was in a bigger city, she had more opportunities to be social.

Unfortunately, little is known about Jane's life between the years 1801 and 1804 because her sister Cassandra destroyed all of Jane's letters from this period. Even though there are hundreds of literature researchers who have painstakingly combed through Jane's life, it is still unclear why her sister would have done this. One thing we do know is that in 1802, Jane received a marriage proposal from family friend Harris Bigg-Wither who came from a wealthy family and was an Oxford-educated man (J.J. Lewis, 2019).

Harris Bigg-Wither has been described as a plain-looking man who spoke with a stutter and lacked tact (Le Faye, 2002). Nonetheless, Jane did accept the proposal, mostly due to practicality. The marriage would ensure that she would be well taken care of, and with her father getting older, it would also help her mother and sister live comfortably (Kennedy, 2019). However, within 24 hours, Jane retracted her acceptance which was a huge blow for both families, who were left embarrassed by her decision (J.J. Lewis, 2019). As there are no surviving letters from this period, there is no straightforward information as to why Jane made this decision, although by examining the contents of her novels, it is clear that Jane was never a big believer in a marriage of convenience.

A Return to Writing

In 1805, tragedy befell the Austen family when the patriarch George Austen died. This became an incredibly difficult time for the three Austen women. Jane's mother, Cassandra Leigh, was left without a penny, as she could not inherit any of her husband's wealth. Her sister, Cassandra, had been engaged to a military man in 1794, sadly he passed away from yellow fever in 1797, leaving her without any financial stability. Jane herself was unmarried, so all three were left in a state of uncertainty. They began to move from house to house, first living with their son and brother Francis Austen and then with Edward Austen. It is estimated that the women lived in at least seven different places between 1805 and 1809, solely depending on the generosity of their male family members to survive (Kennedy, 2019).

The Austen women eventually settled back into Edward's home in Chawton in 1809. Chawton was a small town and lacked a social scene. Jane took this opportunity to return to her passion and spent her time refining *Sense and Sensibility*, *Pride and Prejudice*, and *Northanger Abbey*. Jane also started to take writing more seriously and began expressing interest in publishing her novels.

"By a Lady"

Writing was not a profession deemed suitable for a lady. It was expected that Jane's ambition should be to get married, even if she was considered "old" at the age of 34. Her plight to get published was seen as a departure from femininity, which was so important at the time (Irvine, 2005). Books written by women were usually published either under a male pseudonym or anonymously, and they made very little money from sales.

Jane was an incredibly smart and self-aware woman. She knew better than anyone what society was like—after all, she had spent years satirizing its conventions. She knew that her name wouldn't appear on her published works, although that didn't deter her. With the help of her brother Henry, her books reached London publisher and bookseller Thomas Egerton, who took a liking to *Sense and Sensibility*. In 1811 it was published, and instead of Jane's name, it named the author as "By a Lady."

The novel was a hit. Not only did the general public love it, young aristocrats were taken with it too (Honan, 1987). Due to their social status, it gained even more popularity. The first run of prints sold out by 1813. It was reprinted, and once again sold well. It is estimated that Jane made approximately £140 from *Sense and Sensibility* (which is about £11,000 today—13,200 USD). For the first time in her life, Jane had her own financial independence.

Due to the success of her first published book, its follow-up, *Pride and Prejudice*, was released in 1813, this time denoting the writer as "by the author of *Sense and Sensibility*." After the novel went through two print runs, Jane made £475, which was twice the amount of her father's annual salary (Irvine, 2005).

In 1814, *Mansfield Park* sold out in less than six months. While there is no exact figure on how much she made from this book, it is believed to be more than her first two books.

Acknowledgment

Jane's books were so popular in England that word started to spread outside of the country. Unbeknownst to her (and without her permission), they were illegally translated into French (King, 1953). The French public longed for stories about romance, and even though her books were quintessentially English and explored English society, they were a hit across the Channel too. For a long time, Jane's books were sold without her approval. However, her French popularity was the reason that, for the first time ever, one of her books was actually published under her name. This happened in 1821 with her novel *Persuasion*—published posthumously.

Back in England, Jane's writing caught the eye of Prince Regent (and future King of England) George IV (Le Faye, 2002). He reportedly had copies of her novels in his royal library, and when he found out that she would be releasing another book, *Emma*, in 1815, he requested that it be dedicated to him. You may think that Jane would see this as a great honor, although the historians who have studied her letters say that she deeply disapproved of him. Her disdain was due to the prince's womanizing, drinking, and lude behavior (Halperin, 1985). Still, he was a monarch, and she had to comply.

In 1816, at age 41, Jane's health began to deteriorate. She continued to push through and kept writing, finishing her book *The Elliots* that same year—later to be retitled *Persuasion*. In January 1817, she began working on *The Brothers* (which would go on to be published posthumously under the name *Sanditon* in 1925, over a century later). Due to her debilitating health, she stopped writing in March, and the book was unfinished, containing only 11 chapters.

Jane passed away in August 1817, most likely from Addison's disease, which resulted in Hodgkin's lymphoma.

Henry and Cassandra

Jane's brother, Henry Austen, was largely the reason that Jane's books were even published in the first place. He was instrumental in ensuring that her novels were sold and that she was paid. He was also the one to reveal her as the author of the books after her death. He has, however, been criticized for misrepresenting his sister's personality. In posthumous publications, he wrote a biographical notice, painting his sister as a "faultless" saint (Kennedy, 2019). Jane's sister and closest confidant Cassandra was enraged by this characterization and went on to release some of Jane's most biting letters (Kennedy, 2019). She wanted the world to know that her sister was witty and brilliant and that she never conformed to the ideals of a "perfect woman." Thanks to Cassandra, we now know what Jane was really like—and I'm sure Jane would be pleased that the world sees her as a satirical and creative genius.

JANE AND ADAPTATIONS

Without even realizing it, you've probably consumed more adaptations of Jane's work than you know. There are many direct portrayals of her stories, like the 1995 BBC series and 2005 film of *Pride and Prejudice*, and numerous popular movies have used her stories as a basis. For example, the 1995 classic *Clueless* is based on the book *Emma*. Perhaps most famously, the 2001 smash hit *Bridget Jones' Diary* (both a book and a film) was a raunchy retelling of *Pride and Prejudice*.

There are at least 30 movies based on Jane Austen's books, not to mention writers and playwrights who have been inspired by her work. Even her life story has been immortalized in film, with Anne Hathaway playing Jane in the 2007 film *Becoming Jane*.

JANE'S LEGACY

Jane Austen wrote some of the most popular books of all time. The themes she explored have spoken to audiences for centuries, and people still relate to her characters and critiques of society. Countless online articles list her as one of the best female authors of all time (and often one of the greatest ever, regardless of gender). As I mentioned, over 30 million copies of her books have been sold worldwide, and universities across the world have dedicated classes to the study of her body of work.

In 2017, Jane Austen replaced Charles Darwin on the £10 note in the United Kingdom. In that same year, a statue in her honor was erected in Hampshire to commemorate the 200th anniversary of her death. In Bath, there is an entire museum dedicated to her life and work, and she is also commemorated on the wall of Poet's Corner at Westminster Abbey. Thousands of tourists have visited her grave at Winchester Cathedral, and people have even paid visits to her home in Chawton just to see where she lived for a period of time.

The most enduring part of Jane's legacy is how she has inspired female authors to keep pushing for recognition. It is widely believed that the

Brontë sisters read Jane's work, and even J. K. Rowling has said, "Jane Austen is the pinnacle to which all other authors aspire" (Dean, 2020). I'm sure that there are countless other women who have picked up a pen and written a story because of Jane.

Jane shows us that recognition isn't everything. Pursuing our passions is more important to our happiness than anything else. If there is something you've been putting off doing because you think it will "go nowhere," look to Jane for inspiration and do it just because it brings you joy.

3

ADA LOVELACE (1815–1852)

THE FIRST COMPUTER PROGRAMMER

More than a century before digital computers were developed, Ada Lovelace published an algorithm that made it possible for all future programmers to develop computer machinery. It's amazing to think that a woman who lived in the 1800s is now considered the first-ever computer programmer. Without her brilliant mind, the world of technology would be eons behind where it is now. Before she even entered her 20s, Ada was considered one of the most brilliant mathematical minds of her time. She had the ability to look at science and math through a different lens in order to contribute to the world of technology like no other. She proved that the intelligence of women should never be discounted; she embraced her talent and ignored negative commentary. Ada was surrounded by male contemporaries who were trying to achieve the same thing as her, and she's the one who changed the world. It's her name that we remember.

Ada Lovelace was born into high society in the early 19th century. While her life was certainly easier than women of a lower class, she arguably experienced even more societal pressure due to her status. As I've said, women at this time were born to serve men. There was little room for women to pursue their passions, and it was commonplace for them to suppress their intelligence to appear more desirable. In Ada's case, her parents desperately wanted a son. A daughter was seen as a burden who would bring little value to the family. If they did have a daughter, parents (particularly mothers) would groom them to become proper ladies so that they could marry well and ensure that the family would remain in good social standing. Additionally, upper-class girls were certainly not expected to work. When it came to the study of mathematics, there were no women (that we know of) who were excelling in the field in England. Outliers like 1740s Italian mathematician Maria Agnesi and 1790s Chinese astronomer Wang Zhenyi weren't commemorated for their work for decades. Any contributions made by women would be attributed to men, so the general consensus was that women and math just didn't mix.

Ada was very lucky in some ways. She was born into a highly well-regarded family. Her mother was incredibly intelligent, and she received a good education. She also had challenges. She was plagued with illnesses, suffered from a gambling addiction, and dealt with erratic mental health. She had a difficult relationship with her parents and lacked love and support.

It's common for women to downplay their struggles because they think that other people have it worse or because they are lucky in some ways—I've been there myself. I've suppressed the mental toll of my challenges because I didn't feel like I had the right to complain. Ada's complex story shows us that we can simultaneously be fortunate and have difficulties in our lives. She also shows us that we have the ability to conquer our challenges and be stronger for it.

When researching her life, I found myself inspired by her resilience. She proved that you aren't defined by your struggles, rather by your talent. Regardless of what you've been through in your past or what you are going through now, you have the strength within you to harness your inner brilliance and show off your innate gifts. We all have something that we are great at, and when we feel like life is too difficult, that greatness is what can pull us up and help us persevere.

A BRIEF HISTORY

Augusta Ada King, Countess of Lovelace, was born on the 10th of December 1815 in London, England. Her father, Lord George Byron, was a poet, and her mother, Lady Anna Isabella Byron, was a well-educated woman—though she never worked or showed off her acumen. Ada was the couple's only legitimate child. She had at least two half-siblings as a result of her father's affairs. Lord Byron repeatedly expressed that he wanted a son (Turney, 1972). He was gravely disappointed when his wife gave birth to a girl, so much so that he ordered Lady Bryon to take their daughter 113 miles away to Lady Byron's parents' house at Kirkby Mallory in Leicestershire when Ada was just five weeks old. A few months later, he signed a deed of separation. While English law stipulated that a father was to have full custody of children after separation, he expressed no desire to have a relationship with his daughter. He died when Ada was eight years old, and there is no proof that they ever saw each other before his passing.

Anna Isabella Byron was left to care for her daughter as a single mother. In the eyes of society, Lady Byron presented herself as a doting mother, although historians have concluded that Ada was primarily raised by her maternal grandmother Judith (Lady Milbanke). This conclusion comes as a result of letters written by Lady Byron, where she crudely refers to Ada as "it" and showed little care for her daughter's welfare (Woolley, 1999).

Ada was a sickly child. By the age of eight, she frequently suffered from debilitating headaches, which affected her vision. At 14, she contracted measles which paralyzed her and left her bedridden for a year. She didn't regain the ability to walk until she was 16, and even then, she had to use crutches.

While she struggled with her health, she received private tutelage. She was given lessons in typical "female" subjects, learning French and Italian and studying music and needlework, unlike most girls of her era, she was also taught mathematics and science. Even though Lady Byron was apathetic toward her daughter, she was the one who insisted on these subjects. She herself had a great mathematical mind which influenced this decision.

From as early as age 12, Ada showed a great interest in these subjects. She became fascinated with the concept of flying and spent hours studying the anatomy of birds and their flight techniques, even building a set of wings from wires and paper (Longley, 2021). At 14, she wrote a book titled *Flyology* that explored how a person could theoretically take flight.

The first recognition of her genius came when she was 17 by her tutor, mathematician Augustus De Morgan, who wrote to Lady Byron to inform her of Ada's intelligence. He said that she was becoming "an original mathematical investigator, perhaps of first-rate eminence" (Longley, 2021).

Though she lived a lonely life with an absent mother and little maternal care, she did find solace in her friendship with another one of her math tutors, Mary Somerville. Mary was a great inspiration to Ada. She was respected in scientific circles and knew many important scientists and mathematicians. Mary introduced Ada to these men, including Charles Darwin, and importantly, Charles Babbage. Ada also became a regular at court events, where she charmed people with her brilliant mind (Turney, 1972). It also helped that she was considered attractive and dainty, often garnering the attention of male suitors.

In 1835 at age 20, Ada married William, 8th Baron King. Between 1836 and 1839, she gave birth to three children: Byron, Annabella, and Ralph Gordan (Longley, 2021). As a result of this marriage, Ada became Countess of Lovelace—hence the name she is known by today. The family had three homes, one in Surrey, one in London, and one on Loch Torridon in Scotland. They were a picture-perfect upper-class family.

Ada could have become just another rich wife who threw parties and entertained guests. That just wasn't her style. She loved studying and learning, and she knew how intelligent she was. What she didn't know was that her talent would change the world.

ADA AND MATHEMATICS

After the birth of her last child, Ada returned to her passion for mathematics. In 1841, she resumed her studies with Augustus De Morgan, who was working at the University College London. The lessons were advanced, and Ada never failed to keep up. Additionally, she kept in regular contact with Charles Babbage. The two would trade ideas and theories about how to advance technology through mathematics. While pregnant with her daughter and tending to her firstborn son, Ada corresponded with Charles about his work on a mechanical calculating device that would go on to be named the Analytical Engine. The device and theorems of its function were in their infancy, and Ada followed the progress of its development with intensity.

While Charles initially had government funding for the mathematical calculator, he lost it after a fallout with the craftsman who was helping him build it (Schlombs, 2022). Using her position as Countess, Ada successfully advocated for the government to continue funding the project. Her next stroke of genius was her idea to introduce the calculator to English audiences. An article about the Analytical Engine had been written in French by Italian mathematician Luigi Menabrea, and it had been published in a Swiss journal that didn't reach the UK. (Schlombs, 2022).

In 1842, Ada began translating the article. It is believed that Charles also asked her to add her own notes to the piece. Ada's notes ended up being twice as long as Luigi Menabrea's article (Schlombs, 2022). She was a more innovative and creative thinker and drew upon different parts of her education to provide additional analytical analysis. She specifically used her knowledge of needlework and embroidery to identify repetitive steps needed to assist with the mathematical equations. Using her knowledge of music, she identified that the numbers being manipulated by the Analytical Engine were similar to musical notes.

Ada wrote a set of instructions and algorithms that would help the machine run. Without her additions, the work of both Charles Babbage and Luigi Menabrea wouldn't have been enough to create a mechanical calculating device. Her innovative method is considered the world's first computer program (Gleick, 2011). Furthermore, this set of notes is why she is regarded as the first computer programmer.

Following her contribution, Ada received high praise and acclaim from her peers. Charles was particularly prolific in celebrating her intelligence. In an 1843 letter, he wrote, "that Enchantress who has thrown her magical spell around the most abstract of Sciences and has grasped it with a force which few masculine intellects (in our own country at least) could have exerted over it" (Longley, 2021).

Poetic Science

Ada referred to her approach to mathematics as "poetic science" (Longley, 2021). She saw math as more than just rigid rules and established calculations. She believed that math had the power to explore "the unseen worlds around us" (Longley, 2021). Her ability to blend mathematics with music, embroidery, poetic writing, and the natural world made her stand out. She was also so incredibly intelligent that it baffled men who never considered that a woman could be smarter than they were.

Another insight of Ada's that contributed to the advancement of technology was her recognition of the difference between computing mechanisms and logical structure. She encouraged collaboration between mathematicians and engineers and believed that without the teamwork of these two branches, it would be impossible to build advanced machines.

Computing specialist Doron Swade wrote about Ada's ability to see beyond what others could, stating (Fuegi & Francis, 2003):

Ada saw something that Babbage in some sense failed to see. In Babbage's world his engines were bound by number. What Lovelace saw was that number could represent entities other than quantity. So once you had a machine for manipulating numbers, if those numbers represented other things, letters, musical notes, then the machine could manipulate symbols of which number was one instance, according to rules.

Another writer notes that Ada's process of having a machine complete "looping" —repeating a set of instructions—is still a staple of computer programming in the modern world (Longley, 2021).

An Early Demise

Beyond her contribution to Charles Baggage's work, Ada did little else in the realm of mathematics. Other than her notes on the Analytical Engine, she never published any additional research. This may have been because she simply didn't need to—she was incredibly wealthy and didn't need to pursue a career in science to make money. However, given how passionate she was, it's more likely that she didn't make any further contributions because her life came to an end at the young age of 37. In 1852, Ada was diagnosed with uterine cancer and died a few months later.

ADA AND CONTROVERSIES

It's impossible to tell Ada's story without delving into the controversies that shaped her life. It would be easy to pretend that she was just a genius who made history with her revolutionary ideas, although that isn't a holistic or accurate depiction of her life. Oftentimes, history ignores the challenges women face to make them appear perfect, although women are complex. and they are allowed to have faults while still being role models.

Ada was actually born into a family of controversy. Prior to her birth, her father, Lord Byron, engaged in an incestuous affair with his half-sister, which resulted in the birth of Ada's half-sister Medora. Ada wasn't told about this until 1841, although in a letter to her mother, she wrote, "I am not in the least astonished. In fact, you merely confirm what I have for years and years felt scarcely a doubt about" (Turney, 1972). She was, however, displeased with her mother for writing to her about it, as such a scandal could unravel her life and ruin her reputation.

In the 1840s, when she was in her mid-20s, Ada reportedly had many affairs with men on the social scene. One noted affair was with the son of an engineer whom she had met during the beginning stages of an abandoned experiment on the calculus of the nervous system. John Crosse and Ada's relationship began in 1844 and likely lasted until the end of her life. John destroyed almost all the letters Ada sent him to hide the relationship, although some survived as evidence of the affair. Moreover, Ada put John in her will, leaving him with the only heirlooms that her father had left her (Woolley, 1999). There is no information about whether her husband knew that this was happening, but historians theorize that the couple had a fairly loose attitude about extramarital relationships (Woolley, 1999).

Also in the 1840s, Ada developed a gambling addiction. Over the course of the decade, she reportedly lost the equivalent of $400,000 betting on horse races (Longley, 2021). Ada initially wanted to resolve this debt on her own. She worked on a complex mathematical formula that she believed would guarantee her the money back if she kept gambling. Given how much she had lost, she had to borrow money from friends, including Charles Babbage. Unsurprisingly, it didn't work, and now she was not only in debt, also owed money to people she was close to. She was determined that it would eventually work out in her favor, and it never did. Much to her disappointment, she had to admit to her husband what had happened, which brought her great shame. He paid back all the debt, and she walked away from gambling altogether.

Mental Illness

While I certainly don't consider mental health issues to be a "controversy," rumors of Ada's mental well-being did cause controversy both during and after her lifetime. Obviously, at the time, her condition wasn't recognized as an illness. Instead, she was described as "mad." She would have frequent mental breakdowns that resulted in her struggling to breathe or eat for hours (ETHW, 2018). When she visited a physician to help her overcome this, she was prescribed addictive drugs such as morphine and heroin. This caused her to get worse, as these drugs induced psychosis, leading to her having delusions. It is believed that this is what caused her gambling addiction and ardent belief that she could beat the gambling system with mathematics. She only came off the drugs once diagnosed with cancer.

The reason her mental health condition is marred in controversy is because men at the time said that she was too unstable to be as smart as people said she was (Swansburg, 2021). They believed that someone erratic and, at times, unreasonable could not be intelligent. This led to male contemporaries attempting to discredit her influence on Charles Babbage's work, stating that they believed she was lying about coming up with the additional notes she wrote (Swansburg, 2021).

ADA'S LEGACY

While her friends in the field acknowledged and praised her contribution to the advancement of computer science, it took centuries for her to receive appreciation from those she didn't know intimately. The first popularized recognition of her work came in 1955 when scientist B.V. Bowden wrote about her in his acclaimed book *Faster Than Thought: A Symposium on Digital Computing Machines* (Longley, 2021). Only then did people start to appreciate what she had accomplished.

In 1980, a high-level computer programming language was named "Ada" by the US Department of Defense in her honor. In 1981, the Ada Lovelace Award was created by the Associate for Women in Computing in the US, and in England, the British Computer Society awards the Lovelace Medal for outstanding contributions to the advancement of computing each year. In 2015, the British government added a photo of both Ada and Charles to all newly issued passports.

Ada Lovelace has become an inspiration for all women interested in science, technology, engineering, and mathematics (STEM). Women in STEM only make up about 28% of the workforce, and this figure is rising each year (American Association of University Women, 2020). She broke the glass ceiling and proved that women can be just as intelligent and influential in the field, providing different perspectives that are essential to the progression of innovation.

Despite her struggles both in childhood and adulthood, Ada believed in her intelligence and used it to never give up on herself. She used what she was good at to keep herself happy and to focus her attention away from her issues and onto something she was passionate about. Ada's story shows that challenges are a part of life, and they don't define you. You choose your own legacy.

4

MARIANNE NORTH (1830–1890)

THE INTREPID TRAVELER

Before the invention of the technicolor camera, people relied exclusively on art to see parts of the world that were unknown to them. Scientists and explorers alike relied on artists to capture discoveries and advance their knowledge of the natural world. This means that without the contribution of artists, natural studies would not have been possible—which makes Marianne North all the more impressive and important. Not only was she a talented artist, she had a keen eye for plant life and knew the importance of accuracy when painting. She defied the conventions of the Victorian era and traveled across the world alone to paint and write about the differences between natural habitats in different countries. She visited 17 countries across six continents over a 14-year period, leaving behind a treasure trove of artworks that are revered to this day. Largely due to her gender, her name doesn't live in infamy, although that doesn't make her any less important. She exhibited bravery and intelligence that her male contemporaries could only dream of possessing.

If you've read the stories preceding this one, you know what was expected of Victorian-era women. They had no freedom and were bred to serve men. Even if a woman had a burning desire to see the world, there were strict rules about how they needed to conduct themselves. First, they needed permission from patriarchal figures in their lives (fathers, husbands, brothers, etc.). They relied on these men to provide funding for any trips, as they seldom had money of their own. While not written into law, women were expected to travel with a male companion, and it was extremely rare that a woman would leave on even a short trip on her own. No matter where they went, they had to be "appropriately dressed" in cumbersome full skirts with little skin showing and were encouraged to give all their cash to their male companion. However, with the first wave of feminism hitting the UK in the 1840s, many women started to step outside of the conventions and travel alone. They were viewed as outcasts and rebels, still the number of female travelers continued to rise over the subsequent decades. Women began writing about the world to great acclaim—one example is Nellie Bly's 1890 book *Around the World in Seventy-Two Days*. For centuries, men had been the adventurers, still the tide was starting to shift. This is not to say that it was common for a woman to embark on a solo journey, and it certainly did become more popular for those who could afford it.

Marianne North's passion for travel started when she was young, and she never wavered from her interest in finding out about the world. She combined this curiosity with her fascination with nature and used her talent as an artist to make a name for herself. She had a singular determination to catalog artwork of new species of plant and insect life and made it her mission to paint everything she saw. She had a distinctive and unconventional artistic style that stood out as bold and impressive. Marianne was a woman who kept her head down and did what she wanted without fanfare. Similar to Jane Austen, she didn't set out to change the world or become a household name—she just did what she wanted for pleasure and self-satisfaction.

Marianne is remembered as an energetic, enthusiastic, and experienced traveler (Tyrrell, 2016). She embraced her interests and took every opportunity given to her with gusto. She embodies the spirit of an intelligent and brave woman and is someone we can all look to for inspiration. It's easy enough to put your passion aside and follow the status quo—although that's never going to bring you happiness or help you grow as a person. Sometimes you need to step outside your comfort zone to find your bliss, and even though it's scary, it's so worth it.

A BRIEF HISTORY

Marianne North was born on the 24th of October 1830 in Hastings, England. Her father, Frederick North, was a politician who became an elected Member of Parliament the year after her birth. Little is known about her mother, Janet North, besides the fact that she was the daughter of a prominent politician who was also an MP. Marianne had two younger siblings, Charles and Catherine.

Due to her father's position, the family lived comfortably and wanted for nothing. As a child, Marianne would brush shoulders with influential and prestigious men. One such man was Sir William Hooker, a famed botanist and botanical illustrator. Her father would take her on trips to Kew, where William lived, and it was here that she developed her interest in plants. She would collect samples of exotic flora that William had on his property and, from an early age, started painting. Marianne was also interested in singing and took vocal lessons, although this was short-lived.

In 1847 at age 17, Marianne went on her first trip abroad. The family traveled through Europe for three years. Over the course of this trip, Marianne's interest in studying botany and painting flora intensified. Sadly, her mother passed away in 1855. Before her passing, she made Marianne promise to never leave her father's side (Tyrrell, 2016).

To overcome the grief of losing Janet, Frederick Hastings took his daughters on yet another trip through Europe that same year. Marianne became even more diligent in her record keeping, writing prolifically in her diary about nature and always keeping a sketchbook on hand.

When her younger sister Catherine married in 1864, she became her father's sole companion. Frederick lost his parliamentary seat shortly after and took this opportunity to travel even more, with Marianne always by his side. There is no evidence to suggest that Marianne was interested in marriage or settling down at all. She was more than happy to go on adventures with her father. In 1865, Marianne and Frederick first visited Switzerland, where she was enamored with the beauty of the country's landscape. Next, they went to Northern Italy before leaving

Europe for the first time to visit Egypt and then Syria, finishing with a long stretch of travel along the Nile.

By age 37, Marianne was an expert traveler and wanted to develop her artistic skills further. She took lessons from Australian colonial artist Robert Hawker Dowling who taught her about oil painting. Interestingly, Robert was better known for painting people, not nature, although Marianne still took away some great knowledge about how to paint in this form.

After taking another trip together through Europe, Frederick fell ill while they visited the Alps in 1869. They returned to Hastings for medical care, unfortunately, it was too late, and Frederick died. This completely rocked Marianne's world, and she was overcome with grief. She had spent her entire life by her father's side, and he was her closest friend. As a result of his passing, Marianne received a large inheritance, and as she was unmarried, how to spend the money was completely up to her. Now 39, she still expressed no desire to find a husband, once saying that marriage turned women into "a sort of upper servant" (Tyrrell, 2016).

Despite spending almost her entire life traveling, it was only once she lost her father that Marianne's story really started.

MARIANNE AND HER WORK

Looking for anything to distract herself from the grief she felt, Marianne decided to throw herself back into travel. In 1871, she sold the family home in Hastings and began using her inheritance to plan a solo trip. She experimented with the idea of finding a travel companion and deemed all the people she knew as unsatisfactory. In some instances, her solo travels were made easier due to her family's standing in the political world. She was able to write letters to ambassadors and ministers all over the world to gain information about their countries and rejected any suggestions that she needed a male escort.

Between 1871 and 1872, Marianne traveled to the United States, Canada, and Jamaica. She then went on to Brazil, where she spent eight months, covering as much of the country as possible. During her time there, she completed more than 100 paintings in an attempt to document everything she saw.

In 1875, she began a two-year journey. She painted unique flora found in California and wrote about her concern that native redwoods were being destroyed rapidly (Riley, 1999). She continued on, visiting Japan for the first time before heading to Borneo, Java, and then Ceylon.

Gaining Popularity

Even though she didn't set out to become an artist, Marianne's work started to garner attention from the art world. During her travels, she had sought out artists whom she admired and subsequently sent them her work. Word of her talent spread, and in 1877, an estimated 512 of her oil paintings were put on display at Kensington Gallery. Her work was heavily praised by critics.

Marianne spent most of 1878 in India, where she produced another 200 paintings. She returned to England the following year and donated this collection to the Royal Gardens at Kew and offered to fund the erection of a gallery to house the pieces. They, of course, accepted the offer and began to build a gallery that same year.

After her friend, the famed Charles Darwin, suggested that she visit the relatively recently colonized Australia, she traveled there in 1880 and produced 300 paintings of the incredibly unique plant life native to the country. She also visited New Zealand on this trip.

Upon her return to her home country, she paid a visit to Charles Darwin at his home in Kent to show him the paintings from Australia. He was so pleased with her work that he wrote to her after to thank her, saying (Tyrrell, 2016):

I am so glad that I have seen your Australian pictures, and it was extremely kind of you to bring call up with considerable vividness scenes in various countries which I have seen, and it is no small pleasure; but my mind in this respect must be a mere barren waste compared with your mind.

Some of her most well-regarded artworks came from her Australia collection, including "Banksia attenuata," "B. grandis," and "B. robur" (Collins et al., 2008). In 1881, The Marianne North Gallery at Kew Gardens officially opened to the public. Marianne was instrumental in the organization and displays at the gallery. She chose how the collection would be presented, and as she funded the creation of the gallery, she was able to ensure that the design she created could not be altered without her approval.

Even though she was now a celebrated artist with her own gallery, Marianne wasn't done with travel. In 1882 at age 52, she embarked on a journey to South Africa, where she stayed for approximately two years. In 1884, she visited the Seychelle Islands. Her final trip came in 1885 when she visited Chile to paint the Araucarias trees. This was the last of her paintings.

Her Last Years

After spending her entire life traveling, Marianne finally settled down in 1886 in Gloucestershire in South West England. Around this time, Marianne reportedly began to experience health issues including loss of hearing and rheumatism (Tyrrell, 2016). She didn't paint in the final years of her life, instead working on her autobiography titled *Recollections and Further Recollections of Happy Life: Being the Autobiography of Marianne North*. In this book, she wrote stories about her experience as a solo female traveler and explored the amazing things she did while exploring new countries, including recollections about scaling cliffs, hiking through the wilderness, and crossing through swamps, all of which were driven by her desire to discover and paint different plant life.

In 1890, Marianne passed away from liver disease, and her sister released her autobiography a few years later.

Marianne and Her Paintings

Not only was Marianne one of very few solo female travelers in the Victorian era, she also challenged traditional painting conventions of botanical art. Watercolor paintings were in fashion at the time, and Marianne broke the mold by experimenting with oil paints instead. This resulted in her pieces being more vibrant and bold than those of her contemporaries. As she had a limited color palette at her disposal while traveling (she needed to pack light), she often sketched her drawings on paper first and added color later so that her work was as accurate as possible (McHale, 2020).

Additionally, plant life was often depicted in isolation. Marianne broke this convention by depicting flora in its natural habitat, often including animals and monuments (such as temples) as a part of her paintings. Marianne was the first person to provide a holistic depiction of nature in foreign lands. This was one of the reasons why her paintings were so popular. Technicolor cameras were not invented until 1932, and all images taken by explorers were in black and white. Marianne was able to create a vibrant and realistic snapshot of remote locations, which greatly interested people in Europe who had never seen the faraway world in color.

It is reported that Marianne was keenly aware of her wealth and resulting privilege and wanted to use her art to educate and inspire those who didn't have the same opportunities to travel (McHale, 2020).

Contributions to Botanical Studies

Marianne was celebrated for the beauty and unique nature of her paintings, and her contribution wasn't limited to the art world. Her determination to go to the world's most remote and nearly inaccessible locations led to numerous botanical discoveries. Botanists at the time studied her work closely to learn more about natural life across the world. Many of the species that she discovered are now named after her, including *Nepenthes northiana* and *Crinum northianum*, both of which she uncovered while in Borneo.

Her work is still observed by researchers today. In 2021, Tianyi Yu, a botanical illustrator who spent some time working at Kew Gardens, began to examine her work to see what else could be learned about plant life. He, along with his supervisors at Kew's herbarium, identified a new plant species found in the Matang Forest in Malaysia, which they had previously encountered, although failed to ascertain the origins of. Tianyi Yu notes that their endeavor to identify the origins was largely due to Marianne's attention to geographic detail (Tarlach, 2022). The researchers from Kew weren't the only ones who had spent years trying to figure out this mysterious plant—and it was thanks to Marianne that they were able to find the answer they needed. The plant was named after her, now called *Chassalia northiana*.

Botanists and ecologists believe that this won't be Marianne's last contribution to science (Tarlach, 2022). Scientists across the world travel to her gallery in Kew to learn more about the natural world, and her contribution to botanical and natural studies will live on for centuries after her explorations.

Additionally, Marianne has also advanced the study of entomology (the study of insects), as she often painted native leaf insects and stick insects.

MARIANNE'S LEGACY

When summarizing his study of Marianne's work, Tianyi Yu said, "Marianne North was a pioneer who achieved both scientific and visual appeal... [Her] paintings are inexhaustible treasure" (Tarlach, 2022). She truly was a pioneer—in more ways than one. She set the precedent that women are more than capable of solo travel, even to the most remote parts of the world. She changed the style in which botanical artwork was painted and made it easier for scientists across many fields to learn about the natural world. She did this all at a time when women weren't respected for their intelligence and talent, although she never let that dampen her enthusiasm for adventure.

Numerous plant species from around the world are named in Marianne's honor, and she is often acknowledged by scientists for her contribution to their research. The Marianne North Gallery at Kew Gardens is the only gallery in England that houses a permanent solo collection of work by a female artist (Rideout, 2014). In 2008, curators at Kew Gardens embarked on a mass restoration of her paintings to ensure they would remain in pristine condition for many years to come.

Marianne's belief in herself can encourage all of us to follow our dreams and pursue our passions. It doesn't matter if people think you can't or shouldn't do it—all you need is to look within and harness your confidence. When you do this, you'll become unstoppable.

.

5

---◆◆---

REBECCA LEE CRUMPLER (1831–1895)

THE FIRST AFRICAN AMERICAN FEMALE DOCTOR

In the past two decades, there has been a worldwide rise in the number of female doctors. In most countries, an estimated 49% of doctors are women (OECD, 2021). This equality in the medical field wouldn't be possible without the contribution of women who pushed for recognition. One of the most important women who fought for the right to be a doctor was Rebecca Lee Crumpler. Not only was she the first female African American doctor of medicine, she was also the first published African American physician. Medical studies have always been (and still are) rooted in the patriarchy, with women's health rarely seen as a priority. Rebecca sought to change that, focusing her studies on maternal and pediatric care. She was a pioneer who didn't allow sexism or racism to stop her from achieving her goals.

Slavery in the United States was not abolished until 1865, when Rebecca Lee Crumpler was 30. She lived nearly half her life in a country that enslaved Black people and treated them as less than human. Luckily, Rebecca lived in both Pennsylvania and Massachusetts, where slavery was abolished, although that certainly didn't mean that racism wasn't a huge issue. Almost all universities didn't allow African American students, with only a handful of African American men gaining a college degree in the early 1800s. Additionally, lower-class women were very rarely given anything other than a basic education, with the first public high school for girls opening in 1826 in Boston and New York (Olsen, 1994). It would be many more years before other cities followed suit. Black women were the most marginalized minority during this time, the ramifications of which still linger in today's society. In the 1850s and 1860s, African American women started to join the White suffrage movement, though their fight for equality fell on deaf ears. State by state, White women were given the right to vote in elections, with a federal law passed by Congress in 1920 that stipulated that it was unconstitutional to suppress White female voters. It wasn't until 1965, nearly half a century later, that Black women were given this same right.

Rebecca was born into an incredibly oppressive world and was forced to spend her entire life proving her intelligence and acumen. While this would have been unbelievably difficult for her, she never wavered or allowed society to determine her worth. She was ignored and often degraded by male colleagues who believed that there was no way a woman could be smart enough to be a doctor. They would openly encourage her patients to disregard her medical opinions, and her prescriptions would be rejected. Rebecca never gained the respect of her male peers, but that didn't faze her. She didn't go into medicine to be respected by sexists—she wanted to help people.

Rebecca is remembered for her ability to look past criticism and persevere no matter what others said about her. Of course, it would be foolish to assume that the disrespect didn't affect her in some way. While she never gave up, the contempt her colleagues felt for her would have taken a mental toll. Despite how far we've come in equality, women—particularly women of color—still frequently experience discrimination due to gender and race. I don't know a single woman who hasn't had to deal with this in one way or another. This is particularly prevalent for women who work in male-dominated fields. It's understandable that sometimes we feel like giving up on our pursuits because it feels like we'll never get the respect that we deserve. However, just like Rebecca, we can harness the hate and turn it into motivation. You may never gain the respect of misogynistic men, and it's vital that you don't let them stop you from achieving your goals. Rebecca's story teaches us that believing in oneself is more important than the acceptance of small-minded men. The only person you need to prove yourself to is you.

A Brief History

Rebecca Davis was born on the 8th of February in 1831 in Delaware. There is little information about her parents, Absolum Davis and Matilda Webber, primarily because she moved to Pennsylvania to live with her aunt at an early age. Most of Rebecca's early life has been lost to history, although what is well documented is how much of an inspiration her aunt was. Her aunt worked as a de facto doctor in the local community, spending her time caring for the ill who couldn't afford medical assistance. Rebecca would often join her aunt as she visited people's homes, and she began to understand how important medical care was for all people.

Rebecca reflected on this early experience, writing, "Having been reared by a kind aunt in Pennsylvania, whose usefulness with the sick was continually sought, I early conceived a liking for, and sought every opportunity to be in a position to relieve the sufferings of others" (Rothberg, 2021).

As a teenager, Rebecca was sent to Massachusetts to attend the West-Newton English and Classical School, which was a prestigious private school that boarded students from around the country. Rebecca's intelligence stood out, and she was called a "special student" by teachers (Markel, 2016)

Rebecca set her sights on becoming a nurse. In 1852 at age 22, she permanently moved to the Charlestown neighborhood of Boston, Massachusetts. In that same year, she met and married laborer and former slave Wyatt Lee, thus changing her name to Rebecca Davis Lee.

Between 1855 and 1860, Rebecca was employed as a nurse, assisting doctors in the local area. She worked as a nurse for five years without any formal training or higher studies. Her aptitude for medicine did not go unnoticed, and she greatly impressed the doctors she worked with—so much so that they recommended her for the New England Female Medical College (now merged with Boston University). This was the first school in the country that provided medical education to women (NPS, 2021). The college's acceptance of women was controversial. Men argued that women were delicate creatures who couldn't handle the pressures of medicine. As I mentioned in Caroline Herschel's story, men also believed that because their brains were bigger, they were inherently more intelligent.

These nonsensical beliefs didn't bother Rebecca, and in 1860, she was accepted into the college. She was the only African American student at the time. Statistics show that in 1860, there were 54,000 doctors practicing in the United States, of which only 300 were women (Laskowski, 2020). All of these women were White.

She had no role models. She had no evidence to prove that an African American woman could be a doctor. That was never going to stop Rebecca.

REBECCA AND MEDICINE

While completing her studies, Rebecca continued to work as a nurse. This wouldn't have been easy as her curriculum was rigorous. She had classes in hygiene, medical jurisprudence, chemistry, anatomy, theory, physiology, and therapeutics (F. Lewis, 2019). Historians have noted that Rebecca had to work harder than any other student. Not only was she a woman, she was an African American woman. She attended all her classes and gave her studies her undivided attention.

Things became even more difficult for Rebecca in 1863. Her husband, Wyatt Lee, became sick with tuberculosis in early 1863. She had to withdraw from college to care for him. He succumbed to his illness a few months later. Rebecca had to reapply to the college and was met with hesitation. The first issue the school expressed was that she had taken off too much time and would not be able to catch up to her cohorts. When some of the school's patrons, who were staunch abolitionists, heard about this, they strongly advocated for Rebecca's readmission (Rothberg, 2021). The second issue was a matter of finances. Rebecca was now a widow without a secondary income to support school fees. Rebecca wasn't going to allow this to impede her studies, so she applied for the Wade Scholarship Fund, a tuition initiative created by anti-enslavement activist Benjamin Wade (F. Lewis, 2019). She was awarded the scholarship and resumed her medical education.

In 1864, at age 33, Rebecca graduated from the medical college as a "Doctress of Medicine." She was officially the first-ever African American female doctor. She was keen to start working and opened a practice in Boston that focused on healthcare for women and children from low socioeconomic families (F. Lewis, 2019).

The following year, Rebecca married Arthur Crumpler and became Doctor Rebecca Lee Crumpler. Arthur was a formerly enslaved man from Virginia who had escaped bondage and fled to the North. He served as a Union Army soldier during the Civil War and then began working as a blacksmith. Their wedding was just two months after the end of the war, and the African American population was trying to adjust to the change.

The Freedmen's Bureau

Rebecca's sole driving force was to help those in need. In the aftermath of the war, she saw that newly freed slaves were in dire need of medical care as well as food and housing. She wanted to maximize the number of people she could help. She and Arthur moved to Richmond, Virginia, where slavery was widespread and therefore had more displaced people than in Boston. Their struggles were compounded by the fact that many White doctors refused to treat African Americans.

Upon arriving in Richmond in 1865, Rebecca began working with missionary and community organizations. She primarily collaborated with the Freedmen's Bureau, which was established to support former slaves in the South. Rebecca saw this as both an opportunity to support people who had no access to healthcare and as a way to advance her medical knowledge. Rebecca wrote about her decision to move, stating that Richmond would be "a proper field for real missionary work, and one that would present ample opportunities to become acquainted with the diseases of women and children" (Rothberg, 2021).

Discrimination

Rebecca had dealt with discrimination all her life, and it was particularly prevalent during her time in Virginia. She had always lived in relatively liberal cities, although now she was in Richmond, a city that had been the capital of the Confederate States of America during the war. People in Richmond were opposed to the liberation of slaves and held the belief that African Americans weren't equal to White Americans. It also didn't help that she was a female doctor. Male doctors would openly mock and criticize her and discouraged White patients from seeking her expertise. They publicly joked that her MD stood for "Mule Driver" (Gates Jr & Higginbotham, 2004). It wasn't just doctors; medical administrators and pharmacists were just as bad. They would frequently misfile her patient notes and repeatedly reject prescriptions written by her. She had to tirelessly go out of her way to ensure her patients were being treated.

On the flip side, there was a rise in African Americans seeking medical training (NPS, 2021). They were encouraged to do so because they could see how poorly White doctors treated their people. Rebecca had proven that it was possible for anyone to become a doctor, and she served as an inspiration for future practitioners.

Back to Boston

In 1869, now 38, Rebecca and Arthur returned to Boston. They moved to Beacon Hill, a predominately African American area, and Rebecca opened a practice that operated from their home. She focused on treating women and children and took on patients regardless of their ability to pay (Rothberg, 2021). In 1870, Rebecca gave birth to a daughter, Lizzie Sinclair Crumpler, who sadly died in infancy.

Though not quite as intense as what she experienced in Richmond, Rebecca still routinely dealt with discrimination. Once again, doctors ridiculed her, and pharmacists made it difficult for her patients to receive their prescriptions. She also had no admitting privileges to local hospitals due to her race (Rothberg, 2021).

Rebecca would go on to treat patients, no matter their background, for another 11 years.

REBECCA AND WRITING

After Rebecca's retirement from medical practice in 1880, she and Arthur moved to the Hyde Park neighborhood of Boston. Rebecca began working on a medical book which she completed in 1883. The book, titled *A Book of Medical Discourses*, was a compilation of notes and observations that she had made over her many years of practice. The book focuses on topics such as pregnancy, nursing, child care, maternal care, and teething. It has been described as the forerunner to the bestselling guidebook *What to Expect When You're Expecting* (Rothberg, 2021).

A Book of Medical Discourses is believed to be the first-ever medical text written by an African American author, male or female (Laskowski, 2020).

Knowing that many women couldn't afford healthcare, Rebecca wrote about the prevention of illness and home remedies. She also included some autobiographical information about her life experience and a chapter about how to ensure a happy marriage.

Beyond 1883, there is little available information on Rebecca's life. She died from fibroid tumors in 1895 at age 64 (Laskowski, 2020).

REBECCA'S LEGACY

Historians theorize that Rebecca never knew that she was the first African American female doctor (Laskowski, 2020). Her passion for medicine was never driven by the need to make history or live in infamy. She just wanted to help people who needed it. Even though this wasn't a motivating factor for her, she created a legacy that has survived long past her lifetime. In 1989, the Rebecca Lee Society was established and was one of the first African American medical societies created for women.

The organization's aim was to encourage and support African American women who wanted to become doctors. At Syracuse University, there is a club called The Rebecca Lee Pre-Health Society that promotes the inclusion of people from diverse backgrounds in medical studies. Rebecca's Beacon Hill home is a stop on the popular Boston Women's Heritage Trail.

Prior to 2020, Rebecca was buried in an unmarked grave. This changed 125 years after her death during a well-attended ceremony when a new headstone was erected. The back of the headstone is inscribed with the following passage: "The Community and the Commonwealth's four medical schools honor Dr. Rebecca Crumpler for her ceaseless courage, pioneering achievements and historical legacy as a physician, author, nurse, missionary and advocated for health equity and social justice" (F. Lewis, 2019).

Countless African American women have pursued medical studies, with Rebecca serving as their guiding light. Her ability to ignore and overcome discrimination was her superpower. She proved that passion is more important than recognition. We can all follow in Rebecca's footsteps and overcome the negativity of others. All we need to do is remember our goals and keep working toward success, regardless of what obstacles stand in our way.

6

---◦◦◦---

BEATRIX POTTER (1866–1943)

AUTHOR, ILLUSTRATOR, NATURALIST, AND CONSERVATIONIST

Growing up, you probably read Beatrix Potter's famous children's book, *The Tales of Peter Rabbit*. The book has never been out of print, has sold 40 million copies worldwide, and has been translated into more than 35 languages (Eccleshare, 2022). That alone is enough to show that Beatrix was an incredibly talented and smart woman, and she did more than write and illustrate; she was also a passionate naturalist and conservationist. She advanced the study of fungi both by studying the organism and also illustrating various kinds to help future scientists with their research. Her donation of 4,000 acres of farmland in the Lake District to a conservation organization helped with the preservation of this area's unique and beautiful nature. She is remembered for her various contributions across her different interests, and she cemented herself as one of the smartest women in history.

As an upper-middle-class woman in the United Kingdom, Beatrix received a high-level education although did not attend university. It was rare for women to be admitted into universities around the country, so educational pursuits for females stopped between ages 16 and 17. It was never the goal to ensure girls were intelligent. They were expected to focus first on getting married, then on having children and tending to their household. It comes as no surprise that men were seen as the smarter sex. They had the ability to attend university and study what they pleased, which gave them a leg up over women. Women were expected to only be engrossed in "feminine" things like dancing and music, and seldom were encouraged to pursue other interests. If they did want to learn about other topics or pursue a career, they were met with sexism and backlash. No matter how smart a woman proved herself to be, most men would still view her as inferior.

While Beatrix was able to achieve great success and wealth in her life, she also had to deal with sexism—particularly when it came to her interest in science. People expected her to stick to writing children's books and drawing illustrations and didn't want her to step outside of the box they put her in. Beatrix's intelligence was underestimated time and time again, although that never stopped her from delving into topics that caught her attention.

Beatrix had a "quite strong and determined personality" (Russell, 2022). She harnessed her determination to follow her interests and ignore the naysayers. Without this grit, she may have never become a household name. Beatrix's story is a reminder that women are multifaceted. We are allowed to have as many passions as we like, and we are certainly allowed to be good at more than one thing. Society may want to pigeonhole you and make you think you can only follow one path, although the world is your oyster. You are allowed to dabble in and delve into whatever your heart desires.

A Brief History

Helen Beatrix Potter was born on the 28th of July 1866 in London, England. Her father, Rupert William Potter, was a barrister who specialized in equity law and conveyancing. Her mother, Helen Leech, came from a wealthy family and cared for the household and children. Beatrix had one sibling, a younger brother named William.

The Potter family was considered upper-middle-class and had a comfortable life living in the London suburb of West Brompton. Despite the comfort, Beatrix had a lonely childhood. She was rarely in the company of other children her age and was educated independently by three governesses. Beatrix's parents were both artistic and had a passion for nature, often taking their children to visit the countryside. Beatrix and her brother kept small animals as pets, including mice, hedgehogs, and bats, and collected insects. They would study and draw the animals and insects, and Beatrix always ensured that all the creatures were well looked after.

The family went on holiday every summer at an estate in Perthshire, Scotland. The first evidence of Beatrix's interest in drawing dates back to 1875, when she was eight years old. A preserved copy of her sketchbook from this time contains drawings of the scenery at the estate and is infused with elements of her imagination (Lear, 2016). Beatrix's parents allowed her and her brother to roam freely outside of the estate, and both children became interested in natural history.

Beatrix had a Scottish nanny who raised her, and it has been theorized that the Potter children rarely spent time with their parents outside of summer holidays (Cavendish, 2016). Her nanny often told her stories about witches and fairies and would read her classic works of literature, such as Sir Walter Scott's *Rob Roy* and *Ivanhoe*. Beatrix became obsessed with storytelling, and her imagination developed as she listened to these tales. Once she learned to read on her own, she would delve into any book she could get her hands on.

At age 14, Beatrix began to write in a diary frequently, recounting stories of her day-to-day life and making observations about the world as she knew it (Lear, 2016). Research into the contents of her diary has provided historians with a personal insight into what British society was like at the time. It's also been noted that Beatrix was intelligent beyond her years, specifically due to her observations of nature.

From this diary, we know that Beatrix was often bored and longed for more independence, frequently expressing the desire to earn money. She also wrote about her relationship with her mother, whom she considered to be a demanding woman (Lear, 2016).

In 1882, the Potter family broke from their tradition of going to Scotland and took their first summer holiday in the Lake District in North West England. This trip impacted Beatrix for the rest of her life. She became instantly entranced by the beauty of the area. Incidentally, she also met Hardwicke Rawnsley on this holiday, who at the time was the vicar of a local town and would go on to become the founding secretary of the Natural Trust. The two bonded over their keen interest in country life.

Most of Beatrix's adolescent and teenage years were spent with her brother, and when William was sent away for further education, she was lonelier than ever before. Despite being an obviously very intelligent young woman, she was not sent to university. As such, Beatrix took it upon herself to further her education. She wanted to develop her artistic abilities and began copying from drawing manuals and studying the works of prolific artists such as J.M.W Turner, John Constable, and Thomas Gainsborough to improve her skills (Kosik, 2018). In later life, Beatrix expressed that being a self-taught artist benefited her, as she believed that formal education "would have rubbed off some of the originality" (Kosik, 2018).

A young Beatrix had no idea what her life would hold. She studied for pleasure and because she wanted to learn about different subjects, primarily focusing on science. She didn't know she would become one of the most recognizable names in literary history.

BEATRIX AND SCIENCE

By age 16, Beatrix became intensely interested in mycology—the study of fungi. For the next 10 years of her life, she would spend her time glued to a microscope and drawing detailed illustrations of fungi life. In 1895, she started to focus her studies on how fungi reproduce and made microscopic drawings of fungus spores. After months of research, she began developing a theory about their germination (Lear, 2016). The following year, she was invited by botanists at Kew Gardens to assist with their studies. It was rare for women to be asked to help male scientists with any research, although Beatrix's family was well-connected, and she leveraged this privilege to further her ambitions.

While at Kew Gardens, Beatrix produced hundreds of detailed botanical drawings to assist with the investigation of the cultivation and growth of fungi (Kosik, 2018). Incidentally, this also helped her develop her artistic abilities. She was encouraged by esteemed Scottish naturalist Charles Macintosh, whom she had met while holidaying in Perthshire, to experiment with her style to develop greater technical accuracy. She began using watercolors in her illustrations, which ultimately led to her becoming a respected scientific illustrator.

Working with botanists opened her mind to different theories, and she began to question the theory of symbiosis that had been developed by German mycologist Simon Schwendener. Beatrix's proposal was that fungi had a more independent process of reproduction than previously outlined (Lear, 2016). In 1897 at age 26, Beatrix wrote a scientific paper called "On the Germination of the Spores of the Agaricineae." She submitted her work to the Linnean Society, the world's oldest biological society and one of the most well-regarded institutions. At the time, women could not present their findings to the society or even enter the buildings where they met, so George Massee, Assistant Director of the Royal Botanical Gardens at Kew, presented the paper on her behalf. While this discrimination infuriated her, she still wanted her theories to be heard.

Beatrix's paper was rejected by the Linnean Society. Officially, this rejection was attributed to insufficient evidence to confirm the new theory, and while that may have been a contributing factor, it is largely believed that the rejection was due to her gender. It stands to reason that this was the case because, in 1997, the Linnean Society issued a posthumous apology to Beatrix for the sexism she encountered in the 1890s (Lear, 2016). The Linnean Society, as well as other organizations, have since evaluated her work and used her research to further the study of mycology. Additionally, her beautiful and accurate drawings of fungi have helped mycologists identify different types of the organism.

All this recognition came a century too late, and a disappointed Beatrix decided to discard her scientific studies and focus on illustrations instead.

BEATRIX AND ARTISTRY

Even while she was working diligently on mycology research, Beatrix found the time to engage with her creativity. Before her time at Kew Gardens, she sent an illustrated letter to the ill son of her former governess Annie Moore, writing and illustrating a story about a rabbit named

Peter. From then on, she would routinely write about Peter Rabbit and his family, creating a tale about how they would have misadventures in Mr. McGregor's garden (Kosik, 2018). The first evidence of the iconic characters dates back to 1893.

As mentioned previously, Beatrix had always been interested in earning her own money. In 1890, she began illustrating Christmas cards and other cards for different special occasions, marking her first commercial success as an artist (Green, 2021). Inspired by her childhood pets, she often drew rabbits and other small animals.

Peter Rabbit

At the turn of the century, Beatrix wrote to Annie Moore and her son, asking to borrow the letters she had sent them. At age 34, she began revising her original work to create a children's book titled *The Tales of Peter Rabbit*. The first iteration of the book was in black and white. In 1901, she started to send her work to publishers, all of whom rejected it. Determined to have her book read by others, Beatrix self-published 250 copies and gifted them to friends and family. A copy miraculously landed on the table of Frederick Warne & Co, one of the publishing houses which had previously rejected it. Managing partner and editor Noman Warne saw the book's potential and began to work with Beatrix to see it published. Norman strongly believed that the illustrations should be in color. Beatrix disagreed. After months of persuasion, she finally agreed to his stipulation and re-illustrated the book using watercolors.

In 1902, *The Tale of Peter Rabbit* was published, and it was an instant bestseller. The publishing house had to produce six more editions within 12 months to keep up with the demand (Kosik, 2018). Due to the success, two more of her books, *The Tale of Squirrel Nutkin* and *The Tailor of Gloucester*, were published the following year. From then on, Beatrix exclusively worked with Norman as her editor.

Merchandising, Love, and Loss

Beatrix didn't set out to become a merchandising pioneer. In 1903, she simply wanted to make a gift for Norman's niece and decided to design and sew a Peter Rabbit doll for her. After it was completed, it dawned on Beatrix that this could be a commercial opportunity. Ever the canny businesswoman, she immediately registered the design with the patent office. This was an historic move, and Peter Rabbit became the world's oldest licensed literary character (Kosik, 2018). This started an avalanche of spinoffs, including other characters being made into dolls, board games based on her books, and even china tea sets embossed with her illustrations. Sharing the profit with the publishers, Beatrix amassed a huge amount of money from these sales.

Norman and Beatrix developed an incredibly close bond, and in 1905, he proposed, and she accepted. This union was fiercely opposed by Beatrix's parents. As an upper-middle-class family, the Potters believed that Norman was an unsuitable fit for their daughter because he was "in trade" (Cavendish, 2016). Beatrix was financially independent though, and therefore outside of their control, so they had no way of stopping the marriage. Unfortunately, it would never come to fruition. Less than a month after proposing, Norman passed away from leukemia.

BEATRIX AND THE COUNTRYSIDE

Prior to Norman's death, the couple had planned to buy a holiday home in Hill Top in the Lake District. They had both made a substantial amount of money from book and merchandise sales, and Beatrix had recently received a small inheritance from an aunt. Overcome with grief and searching for solace, Beatrix purchased a farm in Hill Top and moved there permanently.

The Lake District had been Beatrix's favorite place since her first visit there as a teenager. She loved being surrounded by nature in the beautiful countryside and opted to distract herself from grief by learning how to farm. She still published several more children's books, although it was no longer her passion.

Over the course of the next few years, Beatrix acquired more and more land and shadowed local farmers to learn about raising livestock; she also honed techniques in fell farming. Once she began raising livestock of her own, she realized that she needed to protect the boundaries of her land. Beatrix sought the advice of local solicitor William Heelis, who was enamored with her. William courted Beatrix for four years, and the pair married in 1913. Once again, her parents disapproved of the match, as William was nothing more than a country lawyer (Kosik, 2018).

The couple moved to a cottage in Near Sawrey, not far from Hill Top. Here, they had 34 acres of land and began raising sheep. As with everything else in her life, Beatrix wanted to be as proficient as possible and, over time, she became an expert breeder of indigenous Herdwick sheep. By 1920, Beatrix was breeding prize-winning sheep (Cavendish, 2016). In 1942, she was appointed as the first female President-elect of the Herdwick Sheep Breeders Association (Lear, 2016).

Conservation and Last Years

Beatrix acquired huge amounts of land in the Lake District and was an outspoken supporter of the National Trust. She used her wealth to prevent property developers from purchasing land, buying up any estates they were interested in. She was passionate about preserving the nature of the countryside and was considered a "formidably tough" woman who was instrumental in the conservation of the area (Cavendish, 2016).

Her last major work was published in 1930. Toward the end of her life, she began to suffer from deteriorating eyesight, which made illustrating near-impossible. She lived out her last years in the countryside and passed away in 1943 after suffering from heart disease and pneumonia.

Beatrix bequeathed 14 farms and over 4,000 acres of land to the National Trust to ensure it would forever be conserved.

BEATRIX'S LEGACY

Beatrix Potter is the ninth best-selling children's book author of all time (Patterson, 2015). She published 23 children's books in her lifetime, and a further three painting books based on her stories. The Tate Gallery and the British Museum both display her illustrations in permanent collections, and her letters and sketches are on display at the Victoria and Albert Museum in London. In the former law offices of her husband, the National Trust has established the Beatrix Potter Gallery.

Over the last 100 years, there have been hundreds of adaptations of Beatrix's work and retellings of her life story. Children all over the world still read the story of Peter Rabbit, and he is one of the most recognizable literary characters in existence.

Beatrix used her intelligence to contribute to science, conservation, literature, and art. She never limited herself to just one interest and gave her all to every endeavor she took on. She provided a blueprint for women to explore whatever they wanted, showing us that science and art aren't mutually exclusive and we can be good at both. If you ever feel anxious about taking up a new interest or hobby, think about how Beatrix followed her desires, and allow her to inspire you to do the same.

7

MARIE CURIE (1867–1834)

FIRST WOMAN TO WIN THE NOBEL PRIZE AND FIRST PERSON TO WIN TWO IN DIFFERENT CATEGORIES

Irrespective of gender, Marie Curie is one of the most famous scientists in the world. She was the first-ever woman to win a Nobel Prize, the first person to win two Nobel Prizes, and the only person to ever be awarded the prize in two different scientific fields. She is remembered for her discovery of polonium and radium, and was the first person to research how tumors could be treated with radiation, advancing the ability to treat cancer patients. Her contribution to physics, chemistry, and medicine are immeasurable, and she is an undying inspiration to female scientists all over the world.

Marie was originally from Poland, which at the time was ruled over by the Russian Empire. For middle-class women like Marie, life was immensely difficult. Women were controlled by the men in their lives and had few opportunities to rise up in society. In the 1870s, women were given the right to access secondary education although could not attend university. Education was expensive and was a luxury commonly only experienced by upper-class women. For those in lower classes, families had to save to send their daughters to school, and the burden of the fees would often prevent girls from pursuing their studies. A shift happened in the 1800s in favor of women, and for the first time, women were able to earn a wage for themselves. They had more financial freedom than females in other European countries and could even own land and inherit money. While this was a step in the right direction, it certainly didn't amount to the makings of a truly equal society. Women were poorly paid and usually worked in exploitative conditions. They were usually only able to find employment as factory workers and domestic servants (Chevalier, 2018). Those who had some education could be teachers or midwives. Marie also lived in France, where female intelligence was minimized, and as a foreigner, she experienced xenophobia.

While she is a household name in the 21st century, Marie's rise to prominence was riddled with challenges. Despite her undeniable intelligence, many of her male contemporaries refused to accept her genius. Even when her contributions were recognized, they were often justified due to her collaboration with her husband. It was hard for these men to believe that a woman could be smart in her own right.

Marie has been described as a "multifaceted woman of uncommon intensity, intelligence and will" (Des Jardins, 2011). She had to display great courage and have strong mental fortitude to accomplish her goals. Her unwavering determination to make change and advance science helped her overcome adversity. As the first female recipient of the Nobel Prize, she didn't have anybody to look to for guidance. All her strength had to come from within. She proved that the loudest person in the room isn't the most intelligent; she kept her head down and worked hard to achieve her goals.

Marie's strength of character can be an inspiration to us all. The road to success and fulfillment is never easy, and there will always be blockades in the way. It's up to us to look at the women like Marie Curie who came before us and use their power to overcome our own challenges.

A Brief History

Maria Skłodowska was born on the 7th of November 1868 in Warsaw, Poland—then part of the Russian Empire. Her father, Władysław Sklodowski, was a mathematics and physics teacher and director of a secondary school for boys. Her mother, Bronisława Skłodowska, was also a teacher at a boarding school for girls. She was the youngest of five siblings.

Prior to Marie's birth, both sides of her family had been involved in a Polish uprising that aimed to restore Polish independence. This resulted in the family losing their property and wealth, sullying their name in turn. Shortly after Marie's birth, her father was fired from his job by Russian supervisors due to his pro-Polish views. Marie's mother had retired from teaching to raise her children, so the family had to take on boarders in their home to earn money.

Marie began attending a boarding school at age 10, and was an outstanding student. That same year, her mother sadly passed away from tuberculosis. Marie went on to excel at secondary school, graduating in 1883. That same year, she began to experience fatigue and chronic nervousness, which historians believe would be diagnosed as depression in the modern age (American Institute of Physics, 2005). She moved to live with relatives of her father in the countryside in order to recover from her issues. She spent a year there, then moved back to Warsaw.

Marie was envious of her older brother Joseph who was enrolled in medical school, and dreamed of receiving a degree of her own. Women were not permitted to attend university, so Marie's father tutored her. His expertise was in math and physics, which Marie was very interested in. She then enrolled in what is called "Flying University" or "Floating University" with her sister Bronisława. This was a Polish-run institution that allowed female students to attend. It was called "flying" or "floating" because the location of classes frequently had to change to avoid being caught by Russian authorities.

Marie and Bronisława made a deal: Marie was going to help her sister move to France to study medicine, and then Bronisława would help her do the same in two years' time. This led to Marie taking a job first as a tutor and then as a governess so that she could fund her sister's studies. When working for the Zorawski family, she fell in love with their son Kazimierz. The two wanted to marry, although Kazimierz's parents forbade the union, as Marie was poor and undistinguished.

In 1890, Bronisława invited her sister to come to Paris. She had recently married a Polish physician and could afford to pay for Marie's travel. Marie declined the offer. She didn't have enough money saved for university tuition just yet. She continued to work as a governess and tutor and spent all her free time educating herself by reading as many books as she could. She also took lessons at the illegal university, where she began her first practical scientific training in a chemistry lab.

A year later, now aged 24, she left Warsaw and moved to Paris. With a clear goal in mind, she enrolled at the Sorbonne (the University of Paris)—one of the most highly regarded universities in the world. She took classes in chemistry, mathematics, and physics (Reid, 1974). She rented a small, dilapidated apartment near the campus and had meager resources, struggling to keep warm in the winter months.

Despite how intelligent she was, Marie struggled to keep up. Her previous education was lacking compared to her fellow French students, and she struggled to keep up with the language. Reportedly, she was so focused on her academic pursuits that she often forgot to eat (Reid, 1974). She dedicated her entire life to ensuring that she could overcome the gaps in her knowledge and match the output of work by her classmates.

Marie's focus and determination bred great results. She completed her first degree in physics in 1893, graduating at the top of her class (Siewierska, 2017).

This was just the beginning of Marie's scientific career. As a 26-year-old new graduate, she had no idea how much more was yet to come.

MARIE AND SCIENCE

Marie started her research career as soon as she graduated. Her first pursuit was to investigate the magnetic properties of various types of steel. Still struggling financially, Marie's research would not have been possible to complete. Fortunately, senior scientists who had taught her at university, including physicist and future Nobel laureate Gabriel Lippmann, pulled some strings, and the Society for the Encouragement of National Industry began to commission her work. Their funding helped, although Marie still didn't have all the resources she required. She was in desperate need of a larger lab and better facilities to accommodate the complex nature of her research.

The funding did, however, allow her to continue studying at the Sorbonne, now pursuing a degree in mathematics. She studied and did independent research at the same time. For some, just one of these pursuits would have been too exhausting to bear, though Marie never complained. Her only issue was the lack of facilities.

Marie expressed her needs to fellow Polish physicist Jozef Wierusz-Kowalski. He was collaborating with French physicist Pierre Curie at the time and invited her to use their lab. Marie and Pierre instantly bonded, drawn together by their shared interest and dedication to science. They grew closer and closer and eventually fell in love.

Pierre first proposed to Marie in 1894, although she did not accept. Marie was homesick for Poland, and over the university's summer break, she returned to Warsaw. Now an established physicist, she believed that she could continue her studies and research in her home country. She applied to Krakow University and was ultimately rejected due to her gender.

Marie and Pierre

Marie's life was at a crossroads. She wanted to stay with her family in Poland, although this meant that she couldn't follow her academic or research pursuits. Ultimately, it was a string of heartfelt letters from Pierre that convinced her to return to Paris (American Institute of Physics, 2005).

As much as Pierre encouraged Marie, she did the same in return. The two continued their studies. While Pierre had been working as a researcher for nearly 15 years, he had never completed a doctorate (American Institute of Physics, 2005). In March 1895, Marie graduated second in her class in mathematics, and Pierre received a doctorate for his research on magnetism. Pierre subsequently became a professor at the Paris Municipal School of Industrial Physics and Chemistry where he had previously worked as a laboratory chief (American Institute of Physics, 2005). The promotion resulted in a higher salary, which helped the pair fund their research.

Later that year, Marie married Pierre. They had a simple civil ceremony as they were both non-religious. Marie was never the type for flashy things, so she wore a dark blue outfit instead of a traditional white dress, and this outfit would go on to become her laboratory outfit for years (American Institute of Physics, 2005).

Science and Motherhood

Marie was a keen observer of the work conducted by other scientists. Based on the discovery of x-rays and how uranium salt released rays similar to x-rays, she narrowed her research to explore the properties of uranium rays. Unlike her fellow male scientists, Marie was not given adequate lab space or resources to assist her. Undeterred, she utilized her husband's position at the Municipal School of Industrial Physics and Chemistry, and was permitted to use a damp and crowded storeroom as her lab (American Institute of Physics, 2005).

She found that previous research into uranium rays was almost nonexistent and had to develop her own methodologies with no reference point to guide her. Marie was an innovative thinker and began using an electrometer to investigate samples. This electrometer had coincidentally been developed by her husband 15 years earlier.

After tireless investigation and hundreds of hours spent in an insufficient lab, Marie developed a hypothesis that would revolutionize the scientific understanding of uranium. Her theory was that "the emission of rays by uranium compounds could be an atomic property of the element uranium—something built into the very structure of its atoms" (American Institute of Physics, 2005).

While deep in the trenches of research, Marie became pregnant and gave birth to her daughter Irene in 1897. Unable to secure funding and living solely on the wages of Peirre's teaching job, Marie also had to start working to support the family and began teaching as well.

Radioactivity

It was common for women to be the sole carers of their children, although Pierre and Marie shared the load of work so that they could both continue working. Without the support of her husband, Marie may have never achieved greatness, and it was fortunate that Pierre believed so strongly in his wife's work, as many men in this era would have expected their wives to be homemakers.

In 1898 a 31-year-old Marie was juggling motherhood and work. Her research was still unfunded, and she was confined to a storeroom laboratory. Regardless of the difficult conditions and additional pressure of a baby, she persisted. Based on her hypothesis about the atomic properties of uranium, she began collecting mineral sample donations from chemists, and she confirmed her hypothesis. Due to the fact that nobody else had uncovered the atomic emissions of uranium or thorium, there was no word to describe the behavior. So, Marie created her own word: radioactivity (American Institute of Physics, 2005).

Pierre abandoned his independent research into crystals to assist her. He could see that his wife's work was revolutionary. Between 1898 and 1902, the Curies published 32 scientific papers, the most notable of which mentioned that exposure to radium destroyed tumor-forming cells (Sarkar, 2017).

First Nobel Prize

In 1900, Marie made history when she became the first female faculty member at the École Normale Supérieur de Sèvres, teaching physics to female students (Quinn, 2019). In 1903, she received her doctorate from the Sorbonne, and she and Pierre were invited to speak at the Royal Institution in London about radioactivity. While it had been Marie who pioneered the research, she was unable to speak at the institution, which forbade the participation of female lecturers. Pierre used his speech to outline how important his wife's contribution had been to this research.

Two years later, in 1903, Marie and Pierre were awarded the Nobel Prize in Physics and shared the accolade with Henri Becquerel, whose work had been the basis of Marie's research. This further cemented Marie's legacy, as she was the first woman to receive a Nobel Prize. However, this historic recognition almost didn't happen. Marie was originally omitted from the nomination. It was thanks to the intervention of panel member Magnus Goesta Mittag-Leffler, a Swedish mathematician known for his advocacy of women in science, who insisted Marie be included alongside her husband for the award (American Institute of Physics, 2005).

Neither Curie attended the Nobel ceremony in Stockholm. Pierre was struggling with health issues, and they both were too busy to travel. They didn't want any publicity and were more inclined to continue their research, although in 1905 were forced to visit Stockholm, as it was required for Nobel laureates to present a speech that outlined their work. Once again, Marie was unable to deliver the lecture, and true to form, Pierre took great care to highlight how important she was to the research.

Thanks to the award money associated with the prize, the Curies were finally able to conduct research in a proper facility. Pierre became the chair of physics at the Sorbonne, and in 1904, Marie gave birth to their second daughter, Eve.

Tragedy and Perseverance

Now established and celebrated scientists, Marie and Pierre continued to work together on different theorems. Everything changed for the Curie family in April 1906 when Pierre was tragically killed after he was struck by a horse-drawn carriage. It was not only a huge blow to Marie, it was also a blow to the scientific world, and she received dozens of letters from colleagues expressing their condolences (American Institute of Physics, 2005).

Marie was initially ardently opposed to returning to work. She only did so after Pierre's brother, Jacques, insisted that her research was too important not to continue. Marie wrote, "Crushed by the blow, I did not feel able to face the future. I could not forget, however, what my husband used to say, that even deprived of him, I ought to continue my work" (American Institute of Physics, 2005).

Later that year, the Sorbonne offered her a teaching position, making her the first-ever female professor at the institute. When accepting the offer, she requested that the university build a world-class laboratory in his name. In 1909, she created the Radium Institute, now called the Curie Institute.

Second Nobel Prize

The road to Marie's second Nobel Prize was not an easy one. In 1911, five years after her husband's death, Marie started to have an affair with fellow physicist Paul Langevin. When the press caught wind of the affair, Marie was portrayed as a homewrecker (Paul was married), and tabloids focused on how she was a foreigner and misrepresented her as Jewish (Goldsmith, 2005). The general French public turned against her. Additionally, some papers falsely reported that the affair had started while Pierre was still alive, and it had driven him to suicide (American Institute of Physics, 2005).

While the French tabloids and the public disparaged Marie's character, the scientific community continued to honor her work. In the same year that the news of the affair broke, Marie was awarded her second Nobel Prize, this time for her work in chemistry. This made her the first-ever person to win two Nobel Prizes.

This should have been a happy moment in Marie's life, although the toll of the scandal affected her greatly, and she was hospitalized with depression and kidney problems just a month after accepting the award. She shied away from public life in the following years, traveling under her maiden name, and moving between England and Poland to avoid further French degradation.

Final Years

In the last decade of her life, Marie continued her research into radioactivity and worked hard to assist future scientists at the Curie Institute. In the 1920s, she traveled to the United States, Brazil, Spain, Belgium, and Czechoslovakia to give lectures on her research.

In 1922, she became a member of the International Committee on Intellectual Cooperation, a branch of the League of Nations. In 1925, she contributed to the foundation of the Warsaw Radium Institute.

It was Marie's exhaustive work with radiation that ultimately led to her death. Little was known about how damaging radiation could be to a person, and the long-term exposure to radiation led to damage to her bone marrow. She passed away in 1934 at age 66.

MARIE'S LEGACY

Marie's unwavering determination to advance scientific studies left an everlasting footprint. Without her work, the treatment of cancer would be significantly less advanced. X-ray machines would not exist without her research. She is largely considered to be the most important woman in science. There are countless institutes around the world named after the Curies. An atomic element, nuclear reactor, radioactive mineral, and micro-satellite are all named in her honor. A mural of her face has been painted on the facade of her birthplace in Warsaw, and a metro station in Montreal is named after her as well. Her face was on the French 500 franc note before the country adopted the euro as currency. In England, the Marie Curie charity cares for terminally ill patients.

Without Marie Curie breaking through the glass ceiling, female scientists would not be as well regarded as they are today. She inspired so many to pursue scientific studies and make a name for themselves. She created a legacy with little fanfare; she never wanted anything more than recognition for her work and the ability to educate others.

Marie's life was never easy. She was often poor, overlooked, and disparaged. She exhibited immersible mental fortitude and continued to work despite the hurdles in her way. She overcame challenges time and time again and left us with an inspirational story that can improve our own lives. No matter what you are going through, and no matter how dire the circumstances seem, your goals can always serve as a catalyst to keep you going. It's okay to have setbacks; all that matters is that you never give up on yourself.

8

MARIA MONTESSORI (1870–1952)

THE MONTESSORI METHOD

If the name "Montessori" is familiar to you, that is because over 22,000 schools in 110 countries have adopted this educational method (Mountain View Montessori, 2015). If you have children of your own, I'm sure that you've come across this methodology. It is extremely popular in the 21st century, and its history dates back to over a century ago when Maria Montessori developed a new way to educate young children. She blended her knowledge of science and education to revolutionize teaching. She was also one of the first women to attend medical school in her native country of Italy and receive three nominations for the Nobel Peace Prize. In addition to all her work with education, Maria was also a women's rights activist and an advocate for equality for all children.

When the Kingdom of Italy was formed in 1861, the rights of women were extremely limited. The number of women in the workforce was at an all-time high by the time Maria was born, although the conditions were abhorrent. Unsurprisingly, there was a tremendous wage gap between female and male workers, and women were mostly confined to working in factories, with very few opportunities in other fields. Due to the prohibition of female voices in political spheres, female factory workers were often exploited. To ensure that they would not be fired and replaced by men, they frequently had to work over 12 hours a day in unsafe environments. Women started to rebel against these conditions, forming the first female-focused labor union in 1902. One of the main reasons as to why women could only work in factories was because they lacked education. By the 1870s, it was common for girls to attend primary and secondary school, although university was usually not an option. It seemed that the tides were shifting when Ernestina Puritz Manasse-Paper became the first woman to graduate from university in 1877, and for the next 50 years, Italian women pursued their interests. It all came to a crashing halt in the 1920s. The fascist movement swept the country, with leader Benito Mussolini spreading the ideology that a woman's only duty was to procreate and be a mother and wife (Victoria De Grazia, 1993). Women were stripped of academic degrees and forced out of work. It wasn't until 1948 that the Italian government introduced a law that stipulated that women had equal rights to men (Betti, 2018).

Maria's life spanned through all these changes in Italian history. Fortunately, she was able to gain an education prior to fascism but then sadly watched as women's rights were dismantled. She saw it as her duty to advocate for equality, even when it was dangerous for her to do so. Additionally, Maria advocated for children living with disabilities. Differently abled children were outcast by society and viewed as a burden. Under fascist rule, this became an even more common view. Maria was lightyears ahead of her time and believed that all children deserve an education and the opportunity to prosper.

To describe Maria, her son Mario recalled her as "a warm-hearted scientist, she never lost sight of the child as an individual and very special human being" (Montessori, 2020). Maria combined her innate kindness and intelligence to change the world. She was never driven by money or recognition. Instead, all she wanted was to help children achieve their dreams.

Maria's methodologies would have never become popular if she hadn't invested time into her goal. She wouldn't have been able to fight for what she believed in without putting in the work. She set a goal and then worked toward it—that's where it all starts. To achieve what you want from life, you need to set yourself a goal. Then, you need to put your heart and soul into it. Maria came up against complication after complication. She had setbacks and missteps, although none of these were enough to deter her. If Maria could do all this, then so can you. Once you set your mind to something, all you have to do is keep following through—even when it feels impossible.

A BRIEF HISTORY

Maria Tecla Artemisia Montessori was born on the 31st of April in Chiaravalle, in what was then called the Kingdom of Italy. Her father, Alessandro Montessori, worked as an official for the Ministry of Finance and supplemented his income by working at a local tobacco factory. Her mother, Renidle Stoppani, didn't work, though was raised in a well-educated family and subsequently was well-educated herself.

Maria was the couple's only child, and she had a close relationship with both her parents. They would spend a lot of time reading to her and talking to her about the world. The family moved around a lot in Maria's early years before settling in Rome. When Maria was six, she started to attend the local elementary school. In the first grade, she was awarded several certificates for excelling in "women's work" subjects (Kramer, 2017).

In 1884 at age 13, she enrolled in a technical school to study a variety of subjects, including accounting, algebra, history, sciences, and Italian. She graduated at 16 and moved on to a secondary technical institute, studying many of the same subjects, before narrowing down her interests to science and mathematics-based classes.

She had a love of learning and didn't want to stop advancing her education after graduating with a certificate in physics and math in 1890. She initially had thought about pursuing a career in engineering, although at the end of her time in secondary school, her aspirations had shifted toward a desire to attend medical school and become a doctor.

Maria's parents agreed that their daughter should continue her studies although wanted her to enter teaching. Medicine was a male-dominated field and viewed by society as an unacceptable path for women. She applied to study at the University of Rome and was initially rejected. Women were not allowed to participate in subjects geared toward medical studies, and the school requested that she change her course of action. Maria may have been kind-hearted, although that didn't stop her from also being plucky and determined. She appealed to Pope Leo

XIII, who endorsed her, and she was subsequently allowed to enroll (Traficante, 2016).

At age 20, she began attending university, taking classes in anatomy, organic chemistry, experimental physics, histology, and botany (Kramer, 2017). She graduated with a diploma in 1892, which allowed her to apply to the school's medical program. Once accepted, she became one of the first-ever women to attend medical school in Italy.

Her male classmates did not make her university life a pleasant experience; they would endlessly harass and ridicule her. The school contributed in making this a difficult time for her as well. She wasn't allowed to enter a lecture hall until all the male students were seated, and she had to have a male escort when she walked to school, much to the chagrin of her already disapproving father (Quest Montessori School, 2020). It was deemed inappropriate for her to practice the dissection of human cadavers with the male students, so she had to complete dissection practice alone and at night. Even with all this difficulty, Maria was awarded an academic prize for excellence in her first year, which led to a local hospital hiring her as an assistant.

In the next few years, Maria narrowed her studies to focus on pediatrics and psychiatry. At the hospital, she consulted in pediatric rooms and in the emergency department. In 1896 at age 26, Maria graduated from the University of Rome as a doctor of medicine (Kramer, 2017).

Armed with a degree and practical consulting experience, Maria was prepared to tackle the medical world.

Maria and Medicine

After graduation, Maria worked with children and conducted research at the University of Rome's psychiatric clinic, where she also worked as a voluntary assistant. She would study the behavior of children with developmental and mental disabilities and monitor their cognitive skills. In 1897, she audited the university's pedagogy lectures and read every study she could on educational theory. That same year, she gave a speech at the National Congress of Medicine and the First Pedagogical Conference, both in Turin, urging institutions to create special classes for children with disabilities (Kramer, 2017).

In 1898, Maria gave birth to her only child, Mario Montessori. The father of her son was Giuseppe Monesano, a fellow doctor. She didn't want to get married, as this would mean she'd have to stop working. So that she didn't have to pause her career, she sent Mario to live with a wet nurse in the countryside. Maria didn't become a prominent figure in her son's life till he was a teenager, and they would go on to have a close relationship.

Maria's advocacy for differently abled children, along with her research, was garnering attention, and in 1899, she was appointed as a councilor for what was known as the National League for the Protection of Retarded Children (it goes without saying that this term has evolved since). She embarked on a two-week national tour to speak before prominent public figures to help spread the message that children with disabilities deserved to have catered education and that teachers needed to be trained to understand their needs.

MARIA AND EDUCATION

Maria had set out to be a practicing doctor but was so passionate about advocating for children with disabilities that she devoted all her time to this endeavor. She was instrumental in the creation of the Orthophrenic School, which opened in 1900, and she was appointed the position of co-director. The first cohort was made up of 64 teachers who studied the causes and characteristics of mental disabilities, psychology, and special methods of education. The school was deemed an immediate success by the government, as well as prominent psychiatrists and educators in Rome. Students began attending the school. These children came from asylums in the city, as well as from ordinary schools that had deemed them as "uneducable" (Kramer, 2017).

Further Studies

In 1902, Maria enrolled at the University of Rome to study philosophy, though, in modern-day circles, this is called the study of psychology. She took classes although was distracted by her independent studies on educational philosophy. She left the university before she could graduate, with her sights set on applying her educational methods to mainstream education rather than just focusing on children with disabilities (Kramer, 2017).

She began to present reports at pedagogical conferences and published four articles on scientific pedagogy between 1903 and 1904. In 1904, she accepted a position as an anthropology lecturer at the University of Rome.

The First Children's House

In 1907, now 37, Maria opened the first-ever Montessori school in the San Lorenzo district of Rome, which was a low-socioeconomic area. It was called "Casa dei Bambini" and admitted children between three and six years of age. Her observations of the children at the school helped her develop the Montessori method. She concluded that when children were placed in an environment catered to their needs, they were more capable of learning. If lessons were designed around the needs of the child, they were more likely to participate and focus.

Maria began to write prolifically about her ideologies and their success, and by 1911, some public schools in Italy and Switzerland adopted her method (Kramer, 2017). Over the next year, schools in a dozen other countries around the world followed suit. Her work was translated into over 10 languages. *The Montessori Method: Scientific Pedagogy as Applied to Child Education in the Children's Houses* became an international best-seller, as did her subsequent 1914 book, *Doctor Montessori's Own Handbook*.

Between 1912 and 1915, Maria gave lectures across Europe and in the United States. In 1917, she moved to Barcelona, where she was joined by her son, his wife, and their four children.

The Rise of Fascism

Maria returned to Italy in 1922 at the request of the government, which wanted her to inspect the progress of the Montessori schools in the country. Prior to his rise to power, Benito Mussolini heard about Maria's education methodology, and the two met to discuss implementing it in all schools. When he took control of Italy in 1925, Mussolini established Montessori training colleges and Montessori institutions.

It seemed that this change in government was a positive thing for Maria. All was going well, then in 1930, Mussolini and Maria came to a head regarding financial support and ideological values. When Maria refused his request to order teachers to take the fascist loyalty oath, she and her son were placed under police surveillance and then under house arrest. They were ultimately forced to leave the country. Montessori schools in Italy were subsequently closed.

Time in India

Maria and Mario spent the next few years living nomadically throughout Europe. In 1939, Maria visited India to give a training course. She briefly returned to Europe the following year, and when Italy declared that it was a German ally in World War II, she and Mario permanently relocated to Madras and Kodaikanal in India. They lived there for the remainder of the war.

The mother and son duo spent their time in India refining the Montessori method. They developed lesson techniques for teachings about the natural world and how to best engage students in learning about zoology, geography, and botany. Maria began to observe the educational needs of all adolescents. In 1946, she wrote her book *Education for a New World* and then *To Educate the Human Potential* in 1947.

While in India, Maria and Mario trained over a thousand Indian teachers (Montessori Australia, 2019).

Maria returned to Europe in 1946 at age 76. She continued to travel, lecture, and write about her methodology. She was nominated for a

Nobel Peace prize for three consecutive years, starting in 1949. Maria died in 1952 after suffering a cerebral hemorrhage.

MARIA'S LEGACY

Maria's methodology changed the world of education. Prior to her intervention, schooling practices had not been altered for years. She spread the message that all children deserve an education and that no child should be excluded from learning. She advocated for women to be accepted into scientific fields and spoke about how they should receive equal pay (Quest Montessori School, 2020).

Montessori schools are now found in every corner of the globe. In 2020, *Time* magazine listed her as one of the top 100 women of the year. They wrote. "in thousands of classrooms around the world, as children work independently to solve math problems with beads and learn the alphabet with sandpaper letters, their activities can be traced back a century to Maria Montessori's radical educational philosophy" (Reilly, 2020).

Maria challenged the patriarchy and persevered in the face of sexism. She dedicated her entire life to proving that her methodology was worth adopting and never stopped researching and advancing her theory. She proved that determination is enough to get your message across. She knew she needed to provide evidence to back up her methods, and she stopped at nothing to gather the proof she needed to change people's minds. If you feel stuck in life, if you feel like you don't know how to achieve your goal, use Maria's tenacity to empower yourself. There is no challenge that is impossible to overcome. You just need to engage with your inner strength and keep doing what you're doing.

9

---◦---

JOAN BEAUCHAMP PROCTER (1897–1931)

THE DRAGON DOCTOR

In the world of herpetology (the study of amphibians and reptiles), Joan Beauchamp Procter is a rock star. She prolifically contributed to the advancement of zoology research and advanced zoo displays and veterinary practices through innovative ideas and fresh perspectives on best practices. Joan worked at various reputable institutions, including the British Museum of Natural History and the Zoological Society of London. She was the first-ever woman to be appointed as the Curator of Reptiles at the London Zoo. Joan sadly lived a very short life, having struggled with chronic health issues. Nonetheless, she used her time wisely and left an everlasting mark on zoology exploration.

In the early 1900s, women in the United Kingdom started to enter the world of science, technology, engineering, and mathematics (STEM). Pioneers like the previously discussed Ada Lovelace were making strides in the push for more female scientists, although their contribution to research was seldom recognized. Historians note that the work of these early female pioneers was credited as assistants to male scientists, and it was common practice for their independent research to be attached to a male name in publications (Higgitt, 2013). Women were often forbidden from presenting their findings to scientific and government bodies and relied on their male counterparts to introduce their theorems and research. An additional reason as to why women didn't present their own work is because they knew it would not be respected. In an act of self-preservation and out of a desire to advance studies, they selflessly allowed their research to be attributed to men, with their names either removed from the work or added as an aside. They also had to fight the pressure to do "women's work." Within scientific fields, women were expected to work as translators or note-keepers—not scientists themselves. Notably, many female scientists were unmarried. If they chose to enter this field, they were viewed as "unattractive, barren spinsters" (Higgitt, 2013). They had to choose between conforming to the societal expectation that after marriage, they would give up their studies, or pursue their research and remain unwed. Without a secondary income from a husband, they had to rely solely on their own salary. This was no easy feat. There was a massive gender wage gap, and the British government didn't introduce an equal pay act until 1970 (Francis-Devine & Ferguson, 2020). Women who wanted to enter STEM had to sacrifice a lot and fight for their voices to be heard.

With this context in mind, Joan's passion for advancing zoological research is clear. She had an early fascination with science which led her to pursuing a career in a male-dominated field. She knew that she might never be recognized for her work, although it wasn't about acclaim for her; it was about dedication to the evolution of the field. She didn't know that she'd be acclaimed, and it never drove her pursuit.

Despite being a sickly child and struggling with chronic health issues throughout her life, Joan never let this stop her. She was supremely intelligent and very brave. She suffered setbacks due to illness, always found a way to keep going. Her early preoccupation with amphibians and reptiles led to greatness, and she used this childhood fascination to spur on her career.

Joan's life story is full of lessons we can all use for inspiration. She shows us that living with chronic illness issues makes life difficult although shouldn't stop us from achieving our goals. She also shows us that our devotion and intelligence can shine through, no matter what others think. If there is something in your life that you are passionate about, there is no hurdle big enough to stop you from engaging with it. The road may be tough, although you are tougher.

A Brief History

Joan Beauchamp Procter was born on the 5th of August 1897 in London. Her father, Joseph Procter, was a stockbroker. Her mother, Elizabeth Procter, was an artist. She had an older sister, Christabel, and grew up in a home with a huge garden. This led to both sisters having an early fascination with natural history. Additionally, their maternal grandfather, William Brockbank, was an amateur botanist and geologist, and the whole family had a shared interest in the natural world.

From age seven, Joan attended Norland Place School. By the time she was 10, she had developed a keen interest in amphibians and reptiles. She started to keep snakes and lizards as pets and began thoroughly researching British reptile life. Her favorite pet was a large Dalmatian lizard, which she took everywhere. She would even bring it to dinner, setting it on the table while the family ate (Kaba, 2020).

At 12, Joan began to experience chronic intestinal health complications, which affected her for the rest of her life. She didn't allow this to hamper her secondary education, though, and went on to attend St Paul's Girls School in Hammersmith. Much to the dismay of her educators, she acquired a young crocodile which she kept as a pet and took it to class with her (Bailes, 2004). She was described as a brilliant student by her educators. She showed great promise, although her studies were often interrupted due to her health issues. Joan dreamed of attending Cambridge University but unfortunately had to abandon her desire as a consequence of her chronic illness.

Even though she was unable to continue her formal studies, Joan's interest in reptiles never wavered. She began to write to scientists and researchers in London about her desire to learn more. Joan's passionate plight caught the eye of the Keeper of Reptiles and Fish at the British Museum of Natural History, George Albert Boulenger, who took her on as his assistant in 1916. As she lacked a university qualification, the role was voluntary, although she reveled in the opportunity to learn from an expert.

After just a year of volunteering as an assistant, Joan began to conduct independent research into the anatomy and habits of reptiles and amphibians. At 19, she wrote her first scientific paper about pit vipers which were native to Central and South America. She presented her findings to the Zoological Society of London. When George Boulenger retired in 1920, she became a Fellow of the Zoological Society and became solely responsible for the reptiles at the museum (Stearn, 1981). The museum paid her a small stipend for her work, and this, paired with financial assistance from her family, helped her continue her research.

By age 20, Joan was making a name for herself in zoological circles. Her intelligence helped her overcome the fact that she wasn't college educated. She was so young, and her career was just starting.

JOAN AND ZOOLOGY

Between 1917 and 1923, Joan wrote a series of scientific papers after researching a variety of amphibians and reptiles. She looked into their behavior and their anatomy and worked on how they should be classified. One of her most notable papers examined a species of an East African tortoise, where she identified that this tortoise is "able to conceal itself in rock crevices because of its flexible carapace" (Kaba, 2020).

In 1923, she began to question previous research on the midwife toad, which she believed was inaccurate due to insufficient material (Koestler, 2016). This led to her looking into other animals collected by the museum and formally describing their nature. She was celebrated for the high quality of her taxonomic (the scientific study of classifying biological organisms) studies and was subsequently made a Fellow of the prestigious Linnean Society of London.

Joan also had an artistic flair. While at the British Museum of Natural History, she created a series of paintings of amphibians and reptiles, which would go on to be sold as postcards at the museum (Kaba, 2020). She also had a talent for drafting and modeling and used this aptitude to build display cases.

The London Zoo

While busily working at the museum, Joan also took on another responsibility. She was contacted by the son of her former mentor, Edward Boulenger, who was developing the new Aquarium at London Zoo. The pair worked side by side for months, building models of aquarium tanks. Joan's artistic ability came in handy once again, and she designed the rockwork and background for the exhibits. At the completion of the aquarium in 1924, Edward became its director. The London Zoo was so impressed by Joan's work that they appointed her as the Curator of Reptiles (Mitchell, 1929). She was the first-ever woman to hold this position at the zoo.

The London Zoo offered Joan significantly more money than the British Museum of Natural History. In a letter she wrote to a fellow herpetologist, she expressed her joy to leave the museum, as she had often experienced sexism while working there (Greene & Fogden, 2000).

Not only was she responsible for the reptile enclosure, Joan also designed rockwork for the other areas of the zoo. In 1926, the zoo commissioned a purpose-built reptile house, and Joan oversaw the creation of the exhibits and curated the floor plan. The Secretary of the Zoological Society noted that "from the beginning to the end it was her house" (Mitchell, 1929).

As an expert on reptiles, Joan saw great potential in a new way to house the creatures. She is recognized for pioneering the use of "Vita-glass," which "enabled the invisible ultraviolet radiation of the sun to be admitted into the building" (Sadar, 2008). This created a healthier environment for the reptiles held in captivity, as they were now able to naturally absorb Vitamin D.

The Dragon Doctor

When the Reptile House opened in 1927, many exotic and dangerous creatures were acquired for the displays. While many feared the unknown animals, Joan took to caring for them with gusto. She became responsible for feeding and handling crocodiles, pythons, and Komodo dragons. She was known to be affectionate and caring with the animals and seemingly had a knack for taming them.

One Komodo dragon, in particular, was Joan's favorite, and she started to treat it as a pet. She would walk it around the zoo, holding it by the tail (Alexander, 2008). She tamed the dragon so well that visitors were able to pet its head without being bitten.

Joan extended her responsibility to the reptiles by also caring for their health. She worked with the zoo's pathologist to assist with identifying diseases the animals were facing.

Acclaim and Death

Joan became somewhat of a celebrity because of her bravery. Newspapers in both the UK and the US published photos of her with the exotic animals. It was rare to see a woman in a role like hers, and even more rare to see a woman handling dangerous creatures with such ease.

While working intimately with the reptiles and amphibians, Joan also continued to write scientific papers which were published in acclaimed books and journals around the world. Her international acclaim and work with herpetology resulted in her receiving an honorary doctorate as a Doctor of Science from the University of Chicago in 1931 (The Linnean Society, 2019).

Joan's chronic health issues caused her to live in constant pain. She kept working despite how difficult it was for her to do so. In the last few months of her life, she became seriously ill and spent her time painting reptiles to occupy her mind. She passed away from cancer in 1931, aged just 31.

JOAN'S LEGACY

Joan Beachamp Procter revolutionized the way zoologists care for reptiles and amphibians. Her affection for the animals showed that they were more than just dangerous creatures and that they deserved to be adequately looked after. A bust of Joan was carved and first exhibited at the Royal Academy of Arts in London before being permanently displayed at the Reptile House at London Zoo. In honor of her work, two species of reptile have been named after her, a tortoise called *"Testudo procterae"* and a snake called *"Buhoma procterae."*

Joan's advanced ideas of how to exhibit reptiles are still used today, and her research is the foundation for many scientific discoveries in the modern era. Her artworks are revered for their beauty and accuracy. Joan didn't allow illness to stop her from working hard. She overcame her lack of formal university education by proving her acumen in other ways. She never allowed her gender to stop her from doing what she wanted and used her passion to drive her career. She is a reminder that no matter what circumstances life throws at you, you always have the power to persevere.

10

---◆---

GRACE HOPPER (1906–1992)

THE FIRST LADY OF SOFTWARE

The formidable Grace Hopper accomplished many things in her life. She is remembered as a pioneer in computer programming and is a celebrated computer scientist. She also served in the military as a United States Navy rear admiral. Without her contribution, the Apollo moon missions would not have been possible. She was the first woman to be recognized as a distinguished fellow of the British Computer Society and was posthumously awarded the Presidential Medal of Freedom. She was also a passionate teacher who wanted generations of students to follow in her footsteps and achieve their own successes.

In the 1930s, there was a rise in women pursuing university degrees in the United States. Women began to earn bachelor's degrees, primarily in arts subjects. There was also a rise in colleges that only admitted female students. The goal of these colleges was to allow women to gain the same education as men without having to fight against the prejudice they would face in co-ed institutions (Gershon, 2015). These colleges were often focused on the liberal arts. While this was a positive shift, men still held the belief that a woman's primary job was to be a caregiver for children. This meant that it was suggested that female students focus on subjects that would help with their caregiver duties and women often took courses in communication, morals and religion, and physical health (Brisbay, 1990). In the wake of the Great Depression, the number of women in the workforce rose by 20% between 1930 and 1940. They took jobs as nurses, teachers, and secretaries. Interestingly, 26 states had laws that prohibited the employment of married women, as they saw it as the role of a man to be the breadwinner in the family (Remy, 2015). The number of women undertaking master's degrees and working in science was low. The work of women in STEM was overlooked for decades to come.

Grace Hopper was among a handful of women who earned a PhD from Yale. She didn't allow the societal pressure of the time to hamper her plight to gain as much education as she could. She was expected to become a mother and caregiver, although Grace marched to the beat of her own drum. She took every opportunity she could to advance her career with little thought given to what was expected of her.

Grace is remembered for her determination and tenacity. She allowed her curiosity and natural talent to guide her. When she was told "no," she kept pushing until she got what she wanted. As the world changed around her, she saw new possibilities to help others and was a passionate teacher.

Grace's many accolades and achievements demonstrate that perseverance is key. She didn't set out to become a household name—all she wanted was to explore her curiosity. She lived through historical events that changed the world and used these to leverage her career. She never allowed hurdles to derail her. We can all take a little inspiration from her.

A Brief History

Grace Brewster Murray was born on the 9th of December 1906 in New York City. Her father, Walter Murray, was an insurance executive. Her mother, Mary Campbell Van Horne, was a homemaker, though she had spent her early life traveling with her father on surveying trips as he worked as a civil engineer, resulting in Mary's love for mathematics. Grace was the oldest of the family's three children.

Both of Grace's parents believed that girls should be as well educated as boys. Mary's father was particularly passionate about education because he wanted his daughters to be self-sufficient, as he wouldn't be able to leave them with a substantial inheritance to live off of (Bellis, 2019). Grace was educated at a preparatory school in New Jersey. From as early as age seven, she was a very curious child. She became interested in figuring out how alarm clocks functioned and took them apart to see their inner workings for herself.

At age 16, Grace applied for Vassar College, although initially failed the Latin exam. She reapplied and successfully became a student there the following year. In 1928, she graduated with a bachelor's degree in mathematics and physics. She went on to study at Yale University, graduating with a master's degree in 1930. That same year, she married Vincent Foster Hopper, a New York University professor.

In 1931, Grace was hired as a mathematics tutor at Vassar. She also resumed her studies, earning a PhD in mathematics from Yale (Norwood, 2019). By 1941, Grace was promoted by Vassar to the position of associate professor. The world also changed that year, as the United States joined World War II. This would subsequently change Grace's life as well.

GRACE AND THE WAR EFFORT

At age 34, Grace tried to enlist in the US Navy. She was initially rejected due to her age, weight, and height. She continued to apply until she was admitted into the Women Accepted for Volunteer Emergency Services (WAVES) in 1943. She trained at the Naval Reserve Midshipmen's School and graduated first in her class the following year. In 1994, she was sent to serve with the Bureau of Ordinance Computation Project at Harvard University as a lieutenant (Howell, 2016).

Grace's team at Harvard was tasked with creating an early prototype of the electronic computer called Mark I (Norwood, 2019). Utilizing her vast knowledge of mathematics and physics, Grace wrote a 500-page Manual of Operations for the Automatic Sequence-Controlled Calculator (Norwood, 2019). The purpose of this paper was to help the team understand the fundamental operating system of the computer. When writing about the reasons as to why the computer may malfunction, she coined the word "bug" to describe the issues, a phrase that is widely used today. She co-authored an additional three papers with the head of the program, Howard Aiken. Along with her extensive research, she was also instrumental in the building process of Mark I, which would go on to be called the Automatic Sequence Controlled Calculator.

In her personal life, she experienced some difficulties. She and Vincent Foster Hopper divorced in 1945 (Green & Laduke, 2009). Grace kept his surname and never remarried.

GRACE AND CONTINUED COMPUTER ENGINEERING WORK

In 1946, World War II ended, and Grace finished her active duty with the US Military. She continued working with her Harvard team as a contractor under the supervision of the Naval Reserve. The Navy leaders could see how vital she was to the initial project and wanted to keep her employed to take advantage of her expertise. She worked at the Harvard Computation Lab for three more years. During this time, she was instrumental in the advancement of the electronic computer model, helping with the creation of two subsequent models, Mark II and Mark III. Her former employers at Vassar wanted her to return to teaching, offering her full professorship, although she turned them down to continue working at Harvard (Williams, 2001).

UNIVAC

In 1949, at age 47, Grace left her contractor position with the Naval Reserve and was employed by the Eckert-Mauchly Computer Corporation. In a controversial move, the company appointed her as a senior mathematician, a role seldom given to women at this time. She oversaw a team that was mostly made up of males and no doubt had some issues with asserting her authority. Grace overcame any objections by using her undeniable talent and understanding of computing systems.

She was tasked with creating the first general-purpose digital computer called the Universal Automatic Computer (UNIVAC). In 1950, UNIVAC was the most competitive electronic computer on the market, as it was more advanced than the Mark models she had previously worked on (Camp, 2004).

Pioneering Computer Code

While working on UNIVAC, Grace began to research the possibilities of developing a new language of programming that used English words. She said (Gilbert & Moore, 1981):

Manipulating symbols was fine for mathematicians although it was no good for data processors who were not symbol manipulators. Very few people are really symbol manipulators. If they are, they become professional mathematicians, not data processors. It's much easier for most people to write an English statement than it is to use symbols. So I decided data processors ought to be able to write their programs in English, and the computers would translate them into machine code.

Ultimately, it was her goal to assist scientists in all fields to be able to understand and write code. She was knocked back by other senior mathematicians, who strongly believed that computers only had the capability to understand arithmetic. After three years of attempting to prove this was possible, her idea was finally accepted. This came after the Eckert-Mauchly Computer Corporation was taken over by the Remington Rand corporation. In 1954, the new company named Grace as a director of automatic programming, a role specifically created for her. She worked with her department to revolutionize programming language. Grace did extensive research on compilers (a program that translates programming source code into machine code) and completed building the first compiler named A-0.

In the modern era, Grace is recognized for her work with code. When President Barack Obama posthumously named her as a recipient of the Presidential Medal of Freedom in 2016, the citation read that "Hopper's work helped make coding languages more practical and accessible" (Office of the Press Secretary, 2016).

In 1959, Grace was appointed as a technical consultant at the Conference of Data System Languages. At this conference, the new computing language she had created was officially recognized and named the Common Business Oriented Language, better known by the acronym

COBOL. It was the precursor for all future developments in coding language.

Grace spent many years lecturing about the importance of COBOL, giving as many as 300 lectures a year (Norwood, 2019).

Return to the Navy

In 1967, now age 65, Grace returned to work for the US Navy as the director of the Navy Programming Language Group. Six years later, she was promoted to the rank of captain. She worked within the Navy's Office of Information Systems Planning department for 10 years and successfully advocated for COBOL to become the Navy's standardized program.

While in this role, she collaborated with the Department of Defence and implemented a standard for testing computing systems. This led to the creation of a bureau forced on standards, now known as the National Institute of Standards and Technology (NIST). She also helped the government transition from relying on large, centralized computers, replacing them with an array of smaller, more reliable computers (McGee, 2007).

Due to her massive contribution to both the military and government, Grace was promoted to Rear Admiral in 1985. She was one of only a few women to achieve this rank (Howell, 2016). Two years later, she was awarded the Defense Distinguished Service Medal by the Department of Defence—this is the highest award given to military personnel who did not participate in combat (Norwood, 2019).

Last Years

Grace retired from the Navy at 79. She was the Navy's "oldest and highest ranking woman commissioned officer on active duty" (Detroit Free Press, 2014).

Despite now entering her 80s, Grace continued to work. She worked at the Digital Equipment Corporation first as a senior consultant and then as the Principal Corporate Consulting Engineer. Her role was to educate future engineers. This aligned well with Grace, as she had a passion for teaching and spent her last years lecturing about computing with the goal of advancing the knowledge of young computer engineers.

Grace lectured all the way up until her death. She passed away in 1992 at age 85 from natural causes.

GRACE'S LEGACY

Grace's work on the UNIVAC was instrumental in the success of NASA's first Apollo mission and all subsequent missions over the last 60 years (Howell, 2016). She made coding and understanding computer language simple for future generations of scientists and engineers alike. She was one of the first women to be recognized for her work in the tech industry, as well as one of the first female high-ranking officers in the US Navy.

To this day, the number of women who undertake computer science studies is low. Only 22% of engineering undergraduate students in the United States are women (Cheryan et al., 2022). However, in the past five years, there has been a gradual push to encourage women to take positions in STEM. There are more scholarships created every year to push equality in the workforce, and some of these scholarships are named after Grace Hopper.

Many modern women work in male-dominated workforces—you may have experienced this yourself. The takeaway from Grace's story is that gender should never be a determining factor when it comes to success. I know it's difficult to fight against the patriarchy and gain respect from chauvinistic men, although that shouldn't stop you from pursuing whatever you want. Let your natural ability and talent guide and empower you.

————•◦•————

11

HEDY LAMARR (1914–2000)

THE MOTHER OF WI-FI

In the 1930s, Hedy Lamarr was considered to be the most beautiful woman in film. She had an illustrious acting career, starring in a handful of popular movies and commanding attention with her stage presence. This would have been enough to cement her name in the history books, although it wasn't what Hedy wanted from life. She thought there was more to life than being beautiful and famous. Behind her stunning appearance was the mind of one of the greatest inventors the world has ever known. She harnessed her intelligence and curiosity to become a pioneer in the tech world. Without Hedy's creative ideas, the invention and progression of Wi-Fi would be decades behind. She might have a star on the Hollywood Walk of Fame, and she was also inducted into the National Inventors Hall of Fame—there is nobody else in history who excelled in such opposing fields quite like Hedy.

The 1930s saw the rise of the starlet. It was the golden age of Hollywood. With more and more women taking on lead roles in film, societal pressure for women to be beautiful was at an all-time high. Despite the rate of female students attending university spiking to the highest point in US history, intelligence remained an unimportant factor in the eyes of men. Men wanted women to be attractive, demure, and without aspiration. Women were forced to be known either for their looks or for their intelligence (Cohen, 2017). They couldn't be known for both. If they chose intelligence, they would be less likely to marry, as a smart woman intimidated men. History had taught men that they were the ones who needed to be intelligent, and they didn't want that to be challenged—especially not by their wives. It was a crossroads for many women and an unfair decision that they had to make.

Hedy Lamarr pushed against the grain. She wanted to be remembered as a multifaceted woman in an age when that was frowned upon. Despite her overwhelmingly successful career as an actress, she knew that there was so much more she could contribute to the world and didn't let anything stop her from deviating from the path set for her.

By all accounts, Hedy was a determined and outspoken woman. Alexandra Dean, an expert on Hedy's life and director of the documentary *Bombshell: The Hedy Lamarr Story*, said, "For Hedy her power was very much in her appearance but what I love about her is that didn't stop her from going home at night and inventing for the pure joy of it, and the pure need of it" (Werft, 2017). At times, Hedy's beauty hampered her pursuit of being seen as an inventor and frustrated her to no end, although it wasn't enough to stop her from doing what she wanted.

As a modern woman, I'm sure that you can relate to some of Hedy's struggles. It often feels like once we choose a path for our lives, be it career, interests, or family life; we get stuck in the mentality that this is all we are allowed to do. As we get older, our aspirations and ideas of what success means naturally evolve, although it can feel too intimidating to deviate from the direction we've grown accustomed to. If there is a change you want to make in your life, no matter how big or small it may be, use Hedy as an inspiration to challenge yourself. You never know where it could lead.

A Brief History

Hedwig Eva Maria Kiesler was born on the 9th of November 1914 in Vienna, Austria. Her father, Emil Kiesler, was the deputy director of a major bank in the city. Her mother, Gertrud "Trude" Kiseler, was a pianist. She was the couple's only child. The family lived comfortably as part of the upper-class society in Vienna.

Hedy was close with both her parents, and her future career was impacted by their interests. From as early as five years old, Emil would take his daughter on walks around the city, teaching her about the inner workings of machines like streetcars and printing presses (Cheslak, 2018). Inspired by her father's curiosity, Hedy began to take apart her music box to understand the mechanics of how it functioned and taught herself how to reassemble it as well.

Her mother was deeply involved in the arts and would take Hedy to concerts and galleries. She also enrolled her daughter in piano lessons and ballet to explore her creativity.

Hedy's beauty was always a part of her life. By the time she was 12, she had won a local beauty contest (Barton, 2010). This led to Hedy becoming interested in film as a potential career, and she started to take acting classes. German director and producer Max Reinhardt is credited for discovering Hedy as an actress, and at 16, she traveled to Berlin to study acting under his tutelage. That same year she was given a small role in the film *Money on the Street*. In 1932, she was cast in the leading role in the film *Ecstasy*.

The film was both controversial and celebrated. An 18-year-old Hedy appeared in sex scenes and brief nude shots. It was banned in the United States and in Germany although achieved critical acclaim throughout the rest of Europe and won an award at the Venice Film Festival.

Her newfound acclaim led to several roles in the theater. She attracted the attention of munitions manufacturer and dealer Fritz Mandl, and they married in 1933. Hedy was only 18 at the time, and Fritz was 33, 15 years her senior. It's not clear why they married, and it is noted that Hedy was unhappy from the start. When reflecting on her marriage, she said (Cheslak, 2018):

I knew very soon that I could never be an actress while I was his wife... He was the absolute monarch in his marriage... I was like a doll. I was like a thing, some object of art which had to be guarded—and imprisoned—having no mind, no life of its own.

The pair were only married for four years, and that short time was excruciating for the ambitious young actress. This was for a few reasons. First, she had to put her career on hold. Second, her husband was a Nazi sympathizer, despite the fact that they both came from a Jewish background. The last thing that frustrated Hedy was that she was forced to play the role of a happy and dutiful wife, hosting Fritz's colleagues in her home. Due to his position as an arms dealer, high-ranking officials would visit the couple. One noteworthy visitor was Italian fascist leader Benito Mussolini. Hedy also wrote that Adolf Hitler attended the home for dinner, although historians debate the validity of this claim due to the fact that they were a Jewish couple and if Hitler did want to buy weaponry, he would send lower-ranking officers (George, 2019). The only good thing that came from this marriage was that Hedy was privy to conversations about military technology, which would go on to advance her career many years later (Musil, 2014).

There are conflicting accounts of what happened next. It is known for certain that Hedy escaped her marriage in 1937. Some say she went to London by "hiring a maid, drugging her, stealing her uniform, and running away" (Miller, 2021). Others say she sewed jewelry into her clothes and took off on a bicycle while her husband was at a party (Friedrich, 1997). Whatever story is true, we know that Hedy made it to London safe and sound.

Now free of the constraints of her marriage, she was able to pursue her acting career. Her act of bravery led to the beginning of a remarkable life.

HEDY AND HOLLYWOOD

While I want to focus primarily on Hedy's contribution to science, it would be remiss of me to ignore her Hollywood career entirely. Due to her success in *Ecstasy*, she already had an established presence in the film scene. Her arrival in London caught the eye of the head of MGM studios, Louis Mayer. He signed her to a contract with the studio and took her to Los Angeles.

Louis began to market Hedy as the "most beautiful woman in the world" (Miller, 2021). To paint the picture, she had "hazy green eyes, jet black hair, full lips, and coy smile" (Miller, 2021). She also had the allure of being a foreign and exotic woman. She was typecast as a femme fatale, and directors were desperate to work with her. Again, this era is referred to as the Golden Age of Hollywood, and competition for starring roles was tough, although not for Hedy. She was in competition with big names like Natalie Wood and Judy Garland and still came out on top.

Hedy's time in Hollywood spanned two decades, starting in 1938 and ending in 1958. Some of her most famous movies include the Oscar-nominated *Algiers* in 1938, *Ziegfeld Girl* in 1941, *Tortilla Flat* in 1942, *The Strange Woman* in 1946, and *Samson and Delilah* in 1949.

Romantic Life

Hedy married six men during her lifetime. After divorcing Fritz Mandle in 1937, she was married to producer Gene Markey between 1939 and 1941, then to British actor John Loder between 1943 and 1947. This was followed by musician Teddy Stauffer from 1951 to 1952. Then, she married oil tycoon Howard Lee in 1953, and they divorced in 1960. Her final marriage was to lawyer Lewis J. Boies from 1963 to 1965.

She had two children with John Loder. Prior to that, she had adopted Gene Markey's son during their marriage—or so the story went. It turns out this son, James, was biologically hers due to an affair she had with her future husband, John, during her second marriage (Hoffmann, 2001).

Arguably, her most important relationship was not with any of the men she married. It was her brief relationship with aviation pioneer Howard Hughes that changed her life.

HEDY AND INVENTIONS

Hedy's fascination with invention and technology intersects with her time as an actress. She grew tired of people praising her for her beauty and famously said, "The brains of people are more interesting than the looks" (Miller, 2021).

She shared her desire to learn more about science and invention with Howard Hughes, who could see that her intelligence was being stifled by her Hollywood career. He started discussing with her his experimentation with aircrafts, took her to his factories to show her the mechanics of building a plane, and gave her some equipment to tinker with while in her trailer between shooting scenes (Cheslak, 2018). Hedy's natural talent and intelligence astonished him. Hedy began to study fish and birds and used this knowledge to design faster wings for Howard's planes. Upon revealing the design, Howard said to her, "you're a genius" (Cheslak, 2018).

Frequency Hopping

In 1940, Hedy met fellow actor and composer George Antheil. After a conversation at a dinner party, the two realized that they shared a passion for invention. World War II had started a year earlier, and Hedy shared with him that "she did not feel very comfortable, sitting there in Hollywood and making lots of money when things were in such a state" (Cheslak, 2018). Hedy wanted to work with George and, in her typical vivacious style, left her number in lipstick on the windshield of his car.

Hedy became consumed with thoughts of the war and wanted to help. She and George discussed at length how disturbed they were over the sinking of the British ocean liner SS City of Benares, which had claimed the lives of 77 children who had been evacuated due to the escalation of the war (Miller, 2021).

Using the information she had picked up when dining with Nazi leaders, Hedy collaborated with George to invent a new communication system for the military that would help them hop between frequencies and result in a safer way to transmit information without the enemy soldiers listening in. It would also assist with guiding torpedos to their target with more accuracy. She called the invention "frequency hopping."

They engineered the system and submitted it for a patent in 1942. That same year they presented their invention to the Navy—which rejected the implementation of the system.

Wi-Fi

Hedy's invention was not adopted by the Navy until the 1960s—at which stage her patent had expired. Hedy was never paid for her work, and it is estimated that she should have earned approximately $30 million for her invention (George, 2019). The Navy did, however, acknowledge her contribution to the advancement of its systems in 1997 (George,

2019). In that same year, she and George won the Pioneer Award from the Electronic Frontier Foundation.

The legacy of her invention made it possible for future engineers to create Bluetooth and GPS technology, along with Wi-Fi (Miller, 2021). She is often credited as the woman who invented Wi-Fi—sometimes called "the mother of Wi-Fi," along with Vic Hayes, nicknamed "the father of Wi-Fi," who used Hedy's work to establish and popularize wireless technology in the 1990s (Bellis, 2012).

Last Years

Hedy lived a complicated life after her career in Hollywood ended. She was arrested for shoplifting in 1966 and again in 1991, with the second arrest resulting in a sentenced year of probation (George, 2019). It's also rumored that she suffered from an addiction to "pep pills," which had first been given to her by studio executives so that she could work longer hours. It's believed that this was why her behavior was often erratic.

By the 1980s, Hedy had become a recluse, settling in Miami. She continued to experiment with inventing, working on a fluorescent dog collar, designing ideas for airliners, and proposing a new kind of stoplight (George, 2019).

Hedy passed away from heart disease in 2000 at age 85. Her ashes were spread in the Vienna Woods by her son.

HEDY'S LEGACY

One of my favorite quotes from Hedy is, "any girl can be glamorous. All you have to do is stand still and look stupid" (Barton, 2010). I think this perfectly sums up her disdain for being considered just a pretty face. Sure, she was an accomplished actress, although there was so much more to her life than that. In 1997, she was the first female recipient of the Invention Convention's Bulbie Gnass Spirit of Achievement Award (Cheslak, 2018). She was also posthumously inducted into the National Inventors Hall of Fame in 2014.

Hedy didn't receive much recognition prior to the 1990s and made no money from her invention. Starting in the 2010s, her legacy has become more widely known, and her contribution to modern-day technology is no longer ignored.

Hedy's story proves that women aren't just one thing. We can be both beautiful and smart at the same time. We are allowed to be good at a variety of things and should never be pigeonholed. Only you can decide what you want out of life—nobody can stop you from flourishing.

12

---◆---

MARIE VAN BRITTAN BROWN
(1922–1999)

INVENTOR OF THE HOME SECURITY SYSTEM

Our final smart woman is the often-overlooked pioneer of home security, Marie Van Brittan Brown. Marie's idea was born from a personal need for better security, and she saw how her innovation could help millions of people across the globe to stay safe and take control of their own life. She didn't have formal engineering training or even work in the security sector. She was a nurse who used her intelligence to think outside the box and developed something that is still used today. Marie is credited for paving the way for modern home security systems, which so many people (perhaps even you) rely on today to feel safe in their homes.

Marie lived in Jamaica, Queens—a borough of New York City. In the 1960s and 1970s, New York was considered to be a dangerous city. In fact, there was even a campaign that targeted tourists, encouraging them to stay away. A common headline ran on widely distributed pamphlets, and newspapers read "Welcome to Fear City" (Baker, 2018). Subsequent materials were published with guidelines on how to make it out of the city alive. New York was considered dangerous and dirty, a stark departure from today's general perception of the city. Nowadays, the Big Apple hosts over 66 million tourists a year from around the world (Reeve, 2022). However, in the mid-1900s, tourists were wary of making their way to the city and knew there was an inherent risk of mugging and attack on the streets if they decided to visit. For residents, they knew that their homes weren't safe. A study shows that a phenomenon called the "invading army" (a group of young criminals) outnumbered the size of the "defending army" (police and security) by three to one (Pinker,

2013). Crime was a huge issue, particularly in low-income areas like Queens. The people who lived in Queens were usually minority groups, such as African Americans, immigrants from Central and South America, and people from Southeast Asia (Malanga, 2015). The police force was more inclined to protect White citizens in Manhattan, and Queens and Brooklyn were low on resources. Additionally, it's impossible to ignore the fact that the police have a tense relationship with the African American community—a legacy that lives on to this day. Generations of African American people have been victimized by the police and have not felt comfortable asking them for assistance. This left thousands of New York locals unprotected and made them easy prey for criminal activity.

Marie, an African American nurse, worked irregular hours and was often home alone. She was keenly aware of the uptick in crime. She spoke to the *New York Times* about how she faced danger "because police were slow in responding to emergencies in their neighborhood" (African American Registry, 2013).

Marie is remembered as a "highly determined and motivated lady" (The African History, 2022). Instead of succumbing to the dangerous realities of her life, she did something to change her situation: She thought outside of the box. Not only that, she saw an opportunity to help others.

Marie's story is a reminder that a victim mentality does not breed results. We all have the power within us to change our circumstances if we think creatively and explore new possibilities. She also shows us that by helping ourselves, we can help others. No matter what you are going through, there is always a way to overcome your issues. You need to embrace your ability to take accountability and use this to spark your problem-solving skills.

A Brief History

Marie Van Brittan was born on the 30th of October 1992 in Jamaica, Queens. There is very little information about Marie's early life and family. Both of her parents were African American. Her father was born in Massachusetts, and her mother was a Pennsylvania local (Hill, 2019). They moved to New York sometime before the birth of their daughter. It is believed that she was their only child.

It is estimated that Marie met and married her husband, Albert Brown, sometime in the late 1950s, when she was in her 30s. She worked as a nurse, and Albert was an electronics technician. They both worked odd hours, and she was often home alone at night.

One writer notes that "Brown didn't always feel safe as she walked through the neighborhood at night, and crime was on the rise with a 32 percent increase between 1960 and 1965 in Queens. Even once she reached their apartment, Brown worried about her safety" (Carlton, 2022). She felt incredibly vulnerable.

Marie and Albert also had two children, Albert Jr. and Norma. This heightened their desire to have more security in their home. As I mentioned before, the family could not rely on the police for protection.

She may have worked professionally as a nurse, although Marie had an inventive mind (Carlton, 2022). She decided to take matters into her own hands and subsequently changed the world of home security systems.

MARIE AND HER INVENTION

Marie's invention started when she began to think about how she could monitor who was at her door if she heard a noise outside her home. She had a vision for how this could work although lacked the technical knowledge to design a system. She took her idea to her husband and used his electrical expertise to conceive of a device that could be attached to the front door of their house.

It was common for households to have peepholes, although going to the door to look at an unannounced visitor posed danger. If the visitor were an intruder, they would know someone was in the house. As a woman, Marie knew that a male criminal could overpower her. She wanted to have a way to view the potential visitor from a safe distance (Carlton, 2022).

In the early 1960s, Marie and Albert began to devise the first-ever home security system. By 1966, they had a completed model.

History journalist Harry Atkins describes the system by writing (Atkins, 2022):

Her home security system comprised four peepholes, a sliding camera, TV monitors and microphones. The camera could move from peephole to peephole and was connected to TV monitors inside the home. Using those TV monitors, the homeowner would be able to see who was at the door, without having to open or physically attend it. Microphones also played a vital part in the system, allowing a vocal exchange with whoever was outside, again without having to open the door and engage in a face-to-face encounter.

Additionally, she designed a radio button that contacted the police in case of an emergency (Carlton, 2022).

Cutting Edge Technology

Marie's invention hinged on the most cutting-edge technology of the 1960s (Carlton, 2022): CCTV. Close-circuit television (CCTV) was developed by the military in the 1940s and was rarely seen outside the context of military action. It is theorized that the use of CCTV was used by medical students to learn procedures at this time although had no other application. With Marie working as a nurse in hospitals, it is possible that she came across the use of CCTV by medical students, which helped her develop her idea.

Patent

In August of 1966, Marie and Albert submitted a patent application for the monitoring system under the name of "Home Security System Utilizing Television Surveillance" (The African History, 2022). Three years later, in 1969, the government approved the patent. It was the first patent of its kind. Marie's name was listed first on the patent, then Albert's, which was unique, as commonly, a man would be billed above a woman.

That same year, *The New York Times* wrote about the invention. Even though the patent listed Marie as the primary inventor, they credited the invention to Albert and "his wife, Marie" (Carlton, 2022). While this took some of the shine away from Marie, history remembers her as the prime inventor.

The New York Times explained the system this way: "with the patented system, a woman alone in the house could alarm the neighborhood immediately by pressing a button, and installed in a doctor's office it might prevent hold ups by drug addicts" (Buck, 2017).

Ahead of Its Time

After the article was published, the public became interested in the security system. Though Marie intended for the system to be used domestically, business owners saw it as a way of protecting their buildings as well.

The Browns personally manufactured the system for their own home, hoping to see further manufacturing as a result, although it did not bear results. Robert McCrie, an emergency management expert at John Jay College of Criminal Justice in Manhattan, attributes the lack of commercial success to the cost of the device, stating, "the cost of installing it would be pretty high" (Hilgers, 2021). This would have come as a great disappointment to Marie, as she specifically wanted to help protect those in her low socioeconomic area, who needed this system more than anyone else. Additionally, it is noted that "as a black woman on her own, it would have been very difficult to sell an idea into what was totally a male business world" (Kelly, 2015).

Marie and Albert worked for years to improve the system, despite never receiving any payment or financial aid for their work.

Groundwork for the Future

While there is no date attributed to this award, many historians and researchers note that Marie's work was recognized when she received an award from the National Scientists Committee (Kelly, 2015).

Unfortunately, Marie did not see her invention's success, as she passed away in 1999 at age 76. It wasn't until the mid-2000s that CCTV became affordable enough for residential consumers (Carlton, 2022). Marie and Albert's original patent has been cited in 35 subsequent home security system patents (Hilgers, 2021). She may not have lived to see her invention succeed, but she left a lasting impact.

Marie's Legacy

In the aftermath of her invention, the home security industry boomed when CCTV became more cost-effective. Home security is now a $4.8 billion industry, and projections show that these figures are set to triple in the next year (Hilgers, 2021). There are now more than 100 million close-circuit camera systems in operation around the world (Buck, 2017).

Marie's invention has been credited for more than just home security. In 2021, Amazon referenced her original patent in their invention of the "wireless speaker devices for audio/video recording and communication devices" (Carlton, 2022).

On a personal note, Marie's inventive outlook was passed onto her daughter, Norma Brown, who has filed 10 patents of her own, primarily focused on improving health care as she herself became a nurse like her mother (Hill, 2019).

Marie's pursuit to invent was not spurred on by dreams of financial success or acclaim although rather out of necessity. She didn't wait around for someone else to figure out a way to help her protect herself and her family—she found a way to do it herself. Her ability to conceive such a sophisticated system is a testament to how intelligent and innovative she was. She saw no limits to her ideas. She also didn't allow her socioeconomic or racial background to impact her desire to create. She showed that there is no roadblock big enough to stop creative thinking. If you want to make something, you should never allow anything to stop you.

CONCLUSION

Despite what the history books say, it was women who shaped the world. Without the contribution of these fascinating and immensely intelligent women, we would be centuries behind in research, engineering, and technology. They paved the foundation for the modern world. While we now have more opportunities to succeed and to be known for our contributions, these women didn't have it as easy. They had to fight for their voices to be heard and knew that their hard work might never be recognized. Still, they persisted. All these women saw that advancement in their fields was more important than acclaim—this certainly isn't the case for many of their male contemporaries. They showed that integrity and determination are ultimately more important to assisting society than praise and admiration.

Now, it's time to change history and demand recognition. We still have a fight on our hands. Globally, women still make 20% less than men for the same work (United Nations, 2022). Our names are still left off reports, studies, and research papers, and men are frequently given credit for our work. We have the power to change this—and our female predecessors are there to serve as an inspiration to keep pushing through inequality.

We can use the story of Caroline Herschel's life to prove that living with a disability does not make us any less capable. Jane Austen teaches us that pursuing our passion is the key to happiness. Women in STEM can look up to Ada Lovelace to combat the challenges of working in a male-dominated industry. Adventurous women can harness the tenacity of Marianne North to step outside of their comfort zone. Racial prejudice is still a huge issue in the modern world, although Rebecca Lee Crumpler proves that self-belief is enough to overcome barriers. Beatrix Potter's story cements the fact that we are never limited to pursuing just one interest—we can do whatever we want. The legacy left behind by Marie Curie reminds us that no matter how challenging times can be, our goals are a catalyst to keep going. Maria Montessori's single-minded determination to shape the world shows that inner strength is all we need to be successful. Jean Beauchamp Procter serves as a reminder that chronic illness is difficult to live with although is a difficulty we can overcome if we are passionate enough. The story of Grace Hopper shows us that our natural ability is more powerful than sexism. The iconic Hedy Lamarr validates the fact that we should never be pigeonholed. Finally, inventive and creative women can look to Marie Van Brittan Brown for inspiration to take accountability for their lives and look at possibilities from a different lens.

The struggles we go through in the course of our lives make us into the powerful women we are today. The stories of these women prove that no barrier is big enough and no challenge is too hard. We have the inner strength to utilize our life experiences to keep going. You don't have to set a goal to change the world. All you need to do is find what makes you happy and fulfilled and then follow your dreams. When someone tells you that you can't do something or if you feel like you'll never be recognized for your work, remember that there is no knowing what legacy you'll leave behind. Stare boldly in the face of naysayers, and remember, your worth is determined only by you.

If you enjoyed this book, I'd appreciate it if you could please leave a rating and review. I'd love to hear which story resonated with you most. This is part of a series of books on inspirational women. If you'd like to learn more about amazing women who changed history, I'd suggest picking up one of my other books in the No Place For A Woman Series click the link or scan the QR Code below. They will provide you with even more tales of tenacious and history-changing women. Thank you for taking the time to voyage through history with me. Until next time!

No Place For A Woman Series

———✄———

Better still, sign up for my newsletter to keep up to date with what is going on and new releases. As a thank you, make sure you claim your bonus copy of *Badass Cowgirls and The Lady Bushranger*

———✄———

ACKNOWLEDGMENTS

Thank you to everyone who helped and supported me to get this book written and published.

You all know who you are: Aliyah, Michelle, Michael, Andrew and of course family and friends both old and new.

.....and of course my beloved Kitty Kids

REFERENCES

African American Registry. (2013). *Inventor Marie Van Brittan Brown born*. African American Registry. https://aaregistry.org/story/inventor-marie-van-brittan-brown-born/

The African History. (2022, January 23). *Marie Van Brittan: The black woman who invented modern security systems - cctv*. The African History. https://theafricanhistory.com/2329

Alexander, J. (2008). *Wonders of animal life*. Concept Publishing Company.

American Association of University Women. (2020). *The STEM gap: Women and girls in science, technology, engineering and math – AAUW : Empowering women since 1881*. AAUW : Empowering Women since 1881. https://www.aauw.org/resources/research/the-stem-gap/

American Institute of Physics. (2005). *Marie Curie and the science of radioactivity*. Web.archive.org. https://history.aip.org/exhibits/curie/curie.pdf

Atkins, H. (2022, July 6). *Marie Van Brittan Brown: Inventor of the home security system*. History Hit. https://www.historyhit.com/who-was-marie-van-brittan-brown/

Bailes, H. (2004). Procter, Joan Beauchamp (1897–1931), herpetologist.

Oxford Dictionary of National Biography.
https://doi.org/10.1093/ref:odnb/73713

Baker, K. (2018, May 11). *"Welcome to Fear City" – the inside story of New York's civil war, 40 years on.* The Guardian; The Guardian. https://www.theguardian.com/cities/2015/may/18/welcome-to-fear-city-the-inside-story-of-new-yorks-civil-war-40-years-on

Barton, R. (2010). *Hedy Lamarr.* University Press of Kentucky.

Bellis, M. (2012). *Love your home wifi? Thank this guy who wrote the book on it.* ThoughtCo. https://www.thoughtco.com/who-invented-wifi-1992663

Bellis, M. (2019). *Math lover from an early age: The younger years of Grace Murray Hopper.* ThoughtCo. https://www.thoughtco.com/the-younger-years-of-grace-murray-hopper-4077488

Betti, E. (2018). Unexpected alliances: Italian women's struggles for equal pay, 1940s–1960s. *Women's ILO, 32,* 276–299. https://doi.org/10.1163/9789004360433_013

Brisbay, E. (1990). College women in the 1930s: The possibilities and the realities. *The Filson Club Historical Quarterly, 64*(1). https://chicagodefender.com/wp-content/uploads/sites/4/2013/08/64-1-3_college-women-in-the-1930s-the-possibilities-and-the-realities_brisbay-erin.pdf

Buck, S. (2017, June 13). *This African American woman invented your home security system.* Medium; Timeline. https://timeline.com/marie-van-brittan-brown-b63b72c415f0

Camp, C. A. (2004). *American women inventors.* Enslow Publishers.

Carlton, G. (2022, December 23). *The little-known story of the Black woman who invented the modern home security system*. All That's Interesting. https://allthatsinteresting.com/marie-van-brittan-brown

Cavendish, R. (2016, July 7). *Birth of Beatrix Potter*. Www.historytoda y.com. https://www.historytoday.com/archive/months-past/birth-beatrix-potter

Cheryan, S., Master, A., & Meltzoff, A. (2022, July 27). *There are too few women in computer science and engineering*. Scientific American. https://www.scientificamerican.com/article/there-are-too-few-women-in-computer-science-and-engineering/#:~:text=Only%2020%20percen t%20of%20computer

Cheslak, C. (2018). *Hedy Lamarr*. DEV: National Women's History Museum. https://www.womenshistory.org/education-resources/biogr aphies/hedy-lamarr

Chevalier, J. (2018, February 22). *Women in 19th century Russia*. Medium. https://juliettech.medium.com/women-in-19th-century-ru ssia-c70eca8ef68e

Clerke, A. M. (2010). *The Herschels and modern astronomy*. Cambridge University Press.

Cohen, A. (2017, November 22). *Why the tragic story of the Hollywood star who invented Wi-Fi still resonates today*. Www.refinery29. com. https://www.refinery29.com/en-us/2017/11/182013/bombshel l-hedy-lamarr-story-review-susan-sarandon

Collins, K., Collins, K., & George, A. S. (2008). *Banksias*. Bloomings Books.

Curcic, D. (2022, October 25). *Jane Austen statistics*. WordsRated. https://wordsrated.com/jane-austen-books-statistics/#:~:text=Over%2 030%20million%20copies%20of

Dean, C. L. (2020, December 16). *What did they say about Jane Austen?* Writers Write. https://www.writerswrite.co.za/what-did-they-say-about-jane-austen/# :~:text=Charlotte%20Bront%C3%AB%20said%3A%20

Des Jardins, J. (2011, October 1). *Madame Curie's passion.* Smithsonian; Smithsonian.com. https://www.smithsonianmag.com/history/madame-curies-passion-74183598/

Detroit Free Press. (2014, February 22). *Grace Hopper: Retirement (15-Aug-86).* Web.archive.org . https://web.archive.org/web/20140222204821/http://www.waterh oles.com/~dennette/1996/hopper/860815.htm

Eccleshare, J. (2022, April 22). *Peter Rabbit turns 100.* PublishersWe ekly.com. https://www.publishersweekly.com/pw/print/20020422/30 115-peter-rabbit-turns-100.html

ETHW. (2018, October 9). *Ada Lovelace.* ETHW. https://ethw.org/A da_Lovelace#:~:text=As%20her%20mother%20feared%2C%20Ada

Fernie, J. D. (2007). Marginalia: The inimitable Caroline. *American Scientist, 95*(6), 486–488. https://www.jstor.org/stable/27859053

Francis-Devine, B., & Ferguson, D. (2020). 50 years of the Equal Pay Act. *Commonslibrary.parliament.uk.* https://commonslibrary.parliam ent.uk/50-years-of-the-equal-pay-act/

Friedrich, O. (1997). *City of nets: A portrait of Hollywood in the 1940's.* University Of California Press.

Fuegi, J., & Francis, J. (2003). Lovelace & Babbage and the creation of the 1843 "notes." *IEEE Annals of the History of Computing, 25*(4), 16–26. https://doi.org/10.1109/mahc.2003.1253887

Gans, A. (2019). *Laura Wade's the watsons, directed by Samuel West, will transfer to the West End*. Playbill. https://www.playbill.com/article/laura-wades-the-watsons-directed-by -samuel-west-will-transfer-to-the-west-end

Gates Jr, H. L., & Higginbotham, E. B. (2004). African American lives. In *Google Books*. Oxford University Press. https://books.google.com.au/books?id=3dXw6gR2GgkC&pg=PA20 0&redir_esc=y#v=onepage&q&f=false

George, A. (2019, April 4). *Thank this World War II-era film star for your Wi-Fi*. Smithsonian; Smithsonian.com. https://www.smithsonianmag.com/smithsonian-institution/thank-wo rld-war-ii-era-film-star-your-wi-fi-180971584/

Gershon, L. (2015, April 1). *The value of women's colleges: A view from the 1930s*. JSTOR Daily. https://daily.jstor.org/value-womens-colleges -view-1930s/

Gilbert, L., & Moore, G. (1981). *Particular passions: Grace Murray Hopper*. Lynn Gilbert Inc. https://www.vassar.edu/stories/2017/assets/images/170706-legacy-of -grace-hopper-hopperpdf.pdf

Gleick, J. (2011). *The information: A history, a theory, a flood*. Vintage Books.

Goldsmith, B. (2005). *Obsessive genius: The inner world of Marie Curie*. W.W. Norton. https://web.archive.org/web/20160505041336/https:/ /books.google.com/books?id=xuYSLk_tHfgC

Green, A. (2021, December 20). Christmas cards designed by a young Beatrix Potter to go on display. *BelfastTelegraph.co.uk*. https://www.belfasttelegraph.co.uk/entertainment/news/christmas-car

ds-designed-by-a-young-beatrix-potter-to-go-on-display/41166546.ht
ml

Green, J., & Laduke, J. (2009). *Pioneering women in American mathematics: The pre-1940 PhD's*. American Mathematical Society ; London.

Greene, H. W., & Fogden, M. (2000). *Snakes: The evolution of mystery in nature*. Univ. of California Press.

Halperin, J. (1985). Jane Austen's lovers. In *Google Books*. Rice University. https://books.google.com.au/books/about/Jane_Austen_s_Love rs.html?id=mV-szQEACAAJ&redir_esc=y

Herschel, C. (1876). *Memoir and correspondence of Caroline Herschel*. Digital.library.upenn.edu. http://digital.library.upenn.edu/women/he rschel/memoir/memoir.html

Higgitt, R. (2013, October 15). Women in science: A difficult history. *The Guardian*. https://www.theguardian.com/science/the-h-word/20 13/oct/15/women-science-history-ada-lovelace-day

Hilgers, L. (2021, March). *A brief history of the invention of the home security alarm*. Smithsonian Magazine. https://www.smithsonianmag.com/innovation/history-home-security -alarm-180977002/

Hill, R. (2019, September 3). *Marie Van Brittan Brown (1922-1999)*. Black Past. https://www.blackpast.org/african-american-history/brow n-marie-van-brittan-1922-1999/

Hoffmann, B. (2001, February 5). *Hedy news: lamarr's son not adopted*. New York Post. https://nypost.com/2001/02/05/hedy-news-lamarrs-s on-not-adopted/

Holmes, R. (2009). *The age of wonder*. Vintage.

Honan, P. (1987). *Jane Austen, her life*. St. Martin's Press New York.

Hoskin, M. (2014). *William and Caroline Herschel: Pioneers in late 18th-century astronomy*. Springer Netherlands.

Howell, E. (2016, December 2). *Grace Hopper: "First lady of software."* Space.com; Space. https://www.space.com/34885-grace-hopper-biography.html

Irvine, R. P. (2005). *Jane Austen*. Routledge.

Kaba, F. (2020, December 10). *Joan Beauchamp Procter*. Www.womensactivism.nyc. https://www.womensactivism.nyc/stories/8059

Kelly, K. (2015, February 13). *Marie Van Brittan Brown: Home security system inventor*. America Comes Alive. https://americacomesalive.com /marie-van-brittan-brown-home-security-system-inventor/

Kennedy, D. (2019, November 15). The tragic real-life story of Jane Austen. *Grunge*. https://www.grunge.com/174474/the-tragic-real-life -story-of-jane-austen/

King, N. J. (1953). Jane Austen in France. *Nineteenth-Century Fiction*, *8*(1), 1–26. https://doi.org/10.2307/3044273

Koestler, A. (2016). *The case of the midwife toad*. Pan Books.

Kosik, C. (2018). *Beatrix Potter*. Www.illustrationhistory.org. https:// www.illustrationhistory.org/artists/beatrix-potter

Kramer, R. (2017). *Maria Montessori: A biography*. Diversion Books. https://books.google.com.au/books/about/Maria_Montessori .html?id=YxxxQgAACAAJ&redir_csc–y

Laskowski, A. (2020, August 7). *Trailblazing BU alum gets a gravestone 130 years after her death*. Boston University. https://www.bu.edu/articles/2020/rebecca-lee-crumpler-first-black -female-physician-gets-gravestone-130-after-death/

Le Faye, D. (2002). *Jane Austen*. Harry N Abrams Incorporated.

Lear, L. J. (2016). *Beatrix Potter, a life in nature*. St. Martin's Griffin.

Lemonick, M. D. (2009). *The Georgian star: how William and Caroline Herschel revolutionized our understanding of the cosmos*. Atlas ; New York, Ny.

Lewis, F. (2019). *Who was the first African-American woman to become a physician?* ThoughtCo. https://www.thoughtco.com/rebecca-lee-cru mpler-biography-45294

Lewis, J. J. (2019, March 2). *Jane Austen, popular novelist of the Romantic period*. ThoughtCo. https://www.thoughtco.com/jane-austen-biogra phy-3528451

The Linnean Society. (2019, March 8). *Joan Beauchamp Procter FLS*. The Linnean Society. https://www.linnean.org/news/2019/03/08/8th-march-2019-joan-bea uchamp-procter-fls#:~:text=Her%20international%20recognition%20l ed%20her

Longley, R. (2021, February 19). *Biography of Ada Lovelace, first computer programmer*. ThoughtCo. https://www.thoughtco.com/ada-lov elace-biography-5113321

Malanga, S. (2015, December 23). *Why Queens matters*. City Journal. https://www.city-journal.org/html/why-queens-matters-12816.html

Markel, H. (2016, March 9). *Celebrating Rebecca Lee Crumpler, first*

African-American woman physician. PBS NewsHour. https://www.pbs.org/newshour/health/celebrating-rebecca-lee-crumpl er-first-african-american-physician

McGee, R. C. (2007, June 13). *My adventures with dwarfs: A personal history in mainframe computers*. Web.archive.org. https://web.archive.org/web/20070613163123/http://www.cbi.umn. edu/hostedpublications/pdf/McGee_Book-4.2.2.pdf

McHale, E. (2020, May 8). *Things you should know about Marianne North*. Kew. https://www.kew.org/read-and-watch/marianne-north-b otanical-artist

Miller, H. L. (2021, October 19). *How Hedy Lamarr and her inventions changed the world*. Leaders.com. https://leaders.com/articles/leaders-s tories/hedy-lamarr-inventions/

Mitchell, P. C. (1929). Centenary history of the Zoological Society of London. In *Google Books*. The Society. https://books.google.com.au/books/about/Centenary_History_of_th e_Zoological_Soci.html?id=kmg_AAAAYAAJ&redir_esc=y

Montessori Australia. (2019). *Biography of Dr. Maria Montessori*. M ontessori.org.au. https://montessori.org.au/biography-dr-maria-mont essori

Montessori, M. (2020). *Mario Montessori "my most unforgettable character."* Montessori150.org. https://montessori150.org/maria-montessori/mario-montessori-my-m ost-unforgettable-character#:~:text=One%20of%20the%20world

Mountain View Montessori. (2015, September 28). *Montessori Around the World*. Mountain View Montessori. https://mvmreno.com/monte ssori-around-the-world/

Musil, S. (2014, November 9). *Happy 100th birthday,*

Hedy Lamarr, movie star who paved way for Wi-Fi. CNET. https://www.cnet.com/tech/mobile/happy-100th-birthday-h edy-lamarr-movie-star-and-wi-fi-inventor/

Norwood, A. (2019). *Grace Hopper.* National Women's History Museum. https://www.womenshistory.org/education-resources/biographie s/grace-hopper

NPR. (2010, March 25). *Biography offers new glimpses of Jane Austen.* NPR; NPR. https://www.npr.org/2010/03/25/125154892/biograph y-offers-new-glimpses-of-jane-austen

NPS. (2021, April 12). *Dr. Rebecca Lee Crumpler.* Www.nps.gov. http s://www.nps.gov/people/dr-rebecca-lee-crumpler.htm

OECD. (2021). *The proportion of female doctors has increased in all OECD countries over the past two decades.* Www.oecd.org . https://www.oecd.org/gender/data/the-proportion-of-female-doctor s-has-increased-in-all-oecd-countries-over-the-past-two-decades.htm

Office of the Press Secretary. (2016, November 16). *President Obama names recipients of the Presidential Medal of Freedom.* Whitehouse.gov . https://obamawhitehouse.archives.gov/the-press-office/2016/11/16/ president-obama-names-recipients-presidential-medal-freedom

Ogilvie, M. B. (2011). *Searching the stars.* The History Press.

Olsen, K. (1994). *Chronology of women's history.* Greenwood Press.

Patterson, A. (2015, April 2). *The 15 (most likely) best-selling authors of children's books.* Writers Write. https://www.writerswrite.co.za/international-childrens-book-day-the -15-most-likely-best-selling-authors-of-childrens-books/

Pinker, S. (2013). Decivilization in the 1960s. *Human Figurations,*

2(2). https://quod.lib.umich.edu/h/humfig/11217607.0002.206/--de civilization-in-the-1960s?rgn=main

Quest Montessori School. (2020, May 1). *Maria Montessori: A woman who flourished in the face of adversity.* Quest Montessori School. https://www.questschool.org/maria-montessori-a-woman-who-flourished-in-the-face-of-adversity/#:~:text=Montessori

Quinn, S. (2019). *Marie Curie: A life.* Plunkett Lake Press.

Redd, N. T. (2012, September 4). *Caroline Herschel biography.* Space.com; Space. https://www.space.com/17439-caroline-herschel.html

Reeve, D. (2022, April 30). *New York City visitor statistics and tourism figures 2022.* Https://Familydestinationsguide.com/. https://familydestinationsguide.com/new-york-city-visitor-statistics-and-tourism-figures/

Reid, R. W. (1974). *Marie Curie.* Collins.

Reilly, K. (2020, March 5). *Maria Montessori: 100 Women of the year.* Time. https://time.com/5792757/maria-montessori-100-women-of-the-year/

Remy, C. (2015, November 19). *Employment of women in the 1930s.* Medium. https://medium.com/the-thirties/employment-of-women-in-the-1930s-5998fd255f5#:~:text=When%20Depression%20hit%2C%20women%20sought

Rideout, R. (2014, April 10). *The radical Victorian lady behind an essential collection of botanical art.* Atlas Obscura. https://www.atlasobscura.com/articles/marianne-north-and-botanic-art

Riley, G. (1999). *Women and nature.* U of Nebraska Press. https://archive.org/details/womennaturesavin0000rile

Rothberg, E. (2021, October 1). *Dr. Rebecca Lee Crumpler*. National Women's History Museum. https://www.womenshistory.org/educati on-resources/biographies/dr-rebecca-lee-crumpler

Russell, A. (2022, March 12). *The secret life of Beatrix Potter*. The New Yorker. https://www.newyorker.com/news/letter-from-the-uk/t he-secret-life-of-beatrix-potter

Sadar, J. (2008). The healthful ambience of Vitaglass: Light, glass and the curative environment. *Architectural Research Quarterly*, *12*(3-4), 269–281. https://doi.org/10.1017/s1359135508001206

Sarkar, S. (2017, November 15). *Remembering science's most inspirational woman*. The Statesman. https://www.thestatesman.com/opinio n/remembering-sciences-inspirational-woman-1502528346.html

Schlombs, C. (2022, December 9). *Ada Lovelace's skills with language, music and needlepoint contributed to her pioneering work in computing*. The Conversation. https://theconversation.com/ada-lovelaces-skills-with-language-music -and-needlepoint-contributed-to-her-pioneering-work-in-computing-1 93930

Siewierska, K. (2017, March 3). *The struggles and contributions of Marie Curie*. Trinity News. http://trinitynews.ie/2017/03/the-struggles-and -contributions-of-marie-curie/

Stearn, W. T. (1981). *A history of the British Museum (Natural History) 1753-1980*. Heinemann.

Stiller, J. (2023). *Women's education in 18th century*. 18th Century History -- the Age of Reason and Change. https://www.history1700s.com/index.php/articles/25-society-and-cult ure/2397-women-s-education-in-18th-century.html

Sutherland, K. (2014). Jane Austen's juvenilia. *The British Library*. https://www.bl.uk/romantics-and-victorians/articles/jane-aust ens-juvenilia

Swansburg, M. (2021, April 10). *Ada Lovelace: The computer scientist you didn't learn about*. Women's Republic. https://www.womensrepublic .net/ada-lovelace-the-computer-scientist-you-didnt-learn-about/

Tarlach, G. (2022, March 29). *A botanical mystery solved, after 146 years*. Atlas Obscura. https://www.atlasobscura.com/articles/marianne-nort h-chassalia-northiana

Traficante, T. (2016, June 8). *Maria Montessori*. Italian Sons and Daughters of America. https://orderisda.org/culture/women/maria-m ontessori/

Turney, C. (1972). Byron's daughter: A Biography of Elizabeth Medora Leigh. In *Google Books*. Scribner. https://books.google.com.au/books? id=eE1aAAAAMAAJ&redir_esc=y

Tyrrell, K. (2016). *Marianne North*. Botanical Arts and Artists. https: //www.botanicalartandartists.com/about-marianne-north.html

United Nations. (2022, September 18). *Closing gender pay gaps is more important than ever*. UN News. https://news.un.org/en/story/2022/0 9/1126901

Victoria De Grazia. (1993). *How fascism ruled women: Italy, 1922-1945*. University Of California Press.

Walton, G. (2014, August 25). *Ideas of female beauty in the 1700 and 1800s*. Geri Walton. https://www.geriwalton.com/ideas-of-female-bea uty-in-1700-and-1800s/

Werft, M. (2017, April 26). *Hollywood star Hedy Lamarr was a genius, but the world only saw her beauty*. Global Citizen. https://www.global citizen.org/en/content/hedy-lamarr-genius-only-seen-for-beauty/

Williams, K. B. (2001). *Improbable warriors*. Naval Inst Press.

Woolley, B. (1999). The bride of science: Romance, Reason and Byron's daughter. In *Google Books*. Macmillan. https://books.google.com.au/b ooks?id=K8-sQgAACAAJ&redir_esc=y

ABOUT THE AUTHOR

CHRISTINE BENNET

Christine Bennet was originally an English and History teacher. While Christine loved to share stories and educate her students, she left teaching to focus on writing. She has always wanted to write a book about some of the topics she taught at school.

> "There are so many women in history who have either been forgotten or never highlighted for the amazing things that they achieved. I find it a fascinating area to write within." Christine Bennet

When Christine is not writing, she loves to spend time in her garden and has a healthy veggie patch. Her pets are very dear to her and follow her around her home, whether she is inside or out. She of course, loves reading, whether it be non-fiction or fiction.

―――※―――

No Place For A Woman is Christine's first non-fiction book series. Each book in the series focuses on inspirational and strong women who made history. There will be many more books to follow, each book focusing on a different area of life.

To find out more about what Christine is up to or to get notified when Christine's books are released, please sign up for her newsletter. As a thank you, you will receive your copy of the bonus novelette, *Badass Cowgirls and The Lady Bushranger.* An intriguing and fun look at outlaws with spirit, as my editor said, "These chapters were a blast".

Also By Christine Bennet

An intriguing and fun look 3 lady outlaws with plenty of spirit.

Want to be inspired to make a difference? Be empowered by these unstoppable women who break down barriers.

Underpaid for her talent. Unappreciated for her genius. Discover stories of pioneering women who rocked the status quo.

Underpaid for her talent. Unappreciated for her genius. Discover stories of pioneering women who rocked the status quo.

Unappreciated for her genius. Overlooked because she's female. Discover the unfathomable improvements these women made to make the world a better place.

Made in United States
Orlando, FL
13 July 2023

35053593R00086